GERMAN HEAVY CRUISERS
VS
ROYAL NAVY HEAVY CRUISERS

1939–42

MARK LARDAS

Bloomsbury Publishing Plc
PO Box 883, Oxford, OX1 9PL, UK
29 Earlsfort Terrace, Dublin 2, Ireland
1385 Broadway, 5th Floor, New York, NY 10018, USA
E-mail: info@ospreypublishing.com
www.ospreypublishing.com

OSPREY is a trademark of Osprey Publishing Ltd

First published in Great Britain in 2021

A catalogue record for this book is available from the British Library.

ISBN: PB 9781472843098; eBook 9781472843104; ePDF 9781472843074;
XML 9781472843081

21 22 23 24 25   10 9 8 7 6 5 4 3 2 1

Artwork by Ian Palmer
Maps by Bounford.com
Index by Angela Hall
Typeset by PDQ Digital Media Solutions, Bungay, UK

Printed and bound in India by Replika Press Private Ltd.

Osprey Publishing supports the Woodland Trust, the UK's leading woodland
conservation charity.

To find out more about our authors and books visit **www.ospreypublishing.
com**. Here you will find extracts, author interviews, details of forthcoming
events and the option to sign up for our newsletter.

Author's dedication
To Ed Raines and Rick Cotton. You showed me how to build better models.
Now you have helped me write a book.

Author's acknowledgements
I would like to thank Rick Cotton, Ed Jablonski and Ed Raines – three fellow
modelmakers, wargamers and naval history buffs – for their help in preparing
this book. During a time when interlibrary loan was shut down, they
generously helped me find material I needed to write this book, including
lending books from their libraries. I also need to thank my oldest son
Nicholas, for an early birthday present of Norman Friedman's *British Cruisers*.

Photographic sources
The following abbreviations indicate the sources of the illustrations used in
this volume:
AC   Author's collection
USNHHC   US Naval History and Heritage Command

Editor's note
In most cases imperial measurements, including nautical miles (NM), knots
(kn) and long tons, have been used in this book. For ease of comparison please
refer to the following conversion table:

1 NM = 1.85km
1yd = 0.9m
1ft = 0.3m
1in. = 2.54cm/25.4mm
1kn = 1.85km/h
1 long ton = 1.02 metric tonnes
1lb = 0.45kg

Front cover, above: The Christmas Day Battle 1940. *Admiral Hipper* fires a
broadside of its main guns at a distant HMS *Berwick*, while its secondary
battery fires at the merchant ships in convoy WS 5A.
Front cover, below: The Christmas Day Battle 1940. HMS *Berwick*, a Kent-
class heavy cruiser, fires a broadside at the *Admiral Hipper*.

Previous page: HMS *Sheffield* in 1939.

CONTENTS

● German Ports
● British Ports
● Neutral Ports
░ German Reich, occupied territories, allies, and dependent states

GREENLAND

ARCTIC OCEAN

Barents Sea ✕✕
(31 Dec 1942)

Barents Sea

Operation *Rösselsprung* ✕✕
(2–5 Jul 1942)

● Altenfjord

Denmark Strait ✕✕
(22–25 May 1941)

Norwegian Sea

SWEDEN

Hvalfjord ●
ICELAND

● Scapa Flow

USSR

IRELAND   GREAT BRITAIN

Kiel ●

Newfoundland

Brest ●

SWITZERLAND

CANADA

KMS *Admiral Hipper* vs HMS *Berwick*
(25 Dec 1940)
✕✕

USA

PORTUGAL   SPAIN

NORTH ATLANTIC OCEAN

Gibraltar ●

Mediterranean Sea

TURKEY

EGYPT

SPANISH SAHARA

Caribbean Sea

VENEZUELA

COLOMBIA

BRITISH GUIANA
SURINAM
FRENCH GUIANA

GAMBIA
PT. GUINEA

Freetown ●
SIERRA LEONE
LIBERIA

GOLD COAST

NIGERIA

FRENCH EQUATORIAL AFRICA

ANGLO-EGYPTIAN SUDAN

UGANDA

PERU

BRAZIL

Ascension Is.

GABON

BELGIAN CONGO

TANGANYIK

BOLIVIA

ANGOLA

NYASALA

NORTHERN RHODESIA

SOUTHERN RHODESIA

CHILE

PARAGUAY

SOUTH-WEST AFRICA

BECHUANALAND

SOUTH ATLANTIC OCEAN

N

UNION OF SOUTH AFRICA

URUGUAY
● Montevideo

✕✕ River Plate
(13 Dec 1939)

ARGENTINA

0   1,000 miles
0   1,000km

INTRODUCTION

When World War II started, battleships were still queens of the sea. In previous 20th-century wars battleships dominated the oceans and decided naval battles. By World War II, with their numbers restricted by treaty, battleships were viewed as too valuable to risk lightly. They spent most of their time in port, waiting for an opportunity worth risking them.

Patrolling the oceans instead fell on cruisers, especially the heavy cruiser, a class of ship that came into being in 1930 with the signing of the London Naval Treaty. They were smaller than battleships. Cruisers were limited by treaty to a maximum 10,000-ton displacement, while battleships were permitted to be built up to 35,000 tons. No limit was placed on the size of guns battleships could carry. Cruisers could mount guns firing shells no larger than 8in. in diameter (and between 1930 and 1938 could be built with guns no larger than 6in.).

Even if weaker than battleships, cruisers were powerful warships. There were also a lot of cruisers. While battleship numbers were limited by the Washington Naval Treaty, the latter placed no limit on the number of cruisers a navy could have. In the 1920s, most navies built as many cruisers as they desired. Only Germany did not participate in the cruiser building race. Defeated in World War I and with limits on the size and number of ships its navy could possess and build by the Treaty of Versailles, Germany could not do so.

Although cruisers were weaker than battleships, they could outrun them. Enthusiasts described cruisers as ships that could defeat anything they could catch, and run from anything that could defeat them. Critics had another description of cruisers: eggshells armed with hammers. To mount a battery of 8in. guns and hold engines powerful enough to outrun battleships while staying within the 10,000-ton weight limit, cruisers sacrificed armour.

OPPOSITE

The locations of the key battles mentioned in this work.

A dramatic shot of an Admiral Hipper-class cruiser in the opening months of World War II. This is a colourized photograph of either *Admiral Hipper* or *Blücher*. (USNHHC)

That meant cruisers had very light armour, often too light to stop shells fired by other cruisers from penetrating – unless the cruiser was built by nations like Japan, and later Germany, which cheated on their treaty obligations. Those nations ignored the limitations, making ships heavier than allowed and allocating the extra weight to increased armour. Even that armour could not keep out a direct hit from an 8in. shell, however.

A battle between two heavy cruisers would be tentative and indecisive, if the ships fought from great distances to avoid risking damage. At long ranges they avoided being hit, but were unlikely to hit anything. Equally, if both sides closed range, seeking a decisive engagement, battle could be bloody. Any hit could potentially cause serious damage. Since gunfire rarely sank a ship, a prolonged exchange yielded two battered cruisers, badly damaged, but still capable of steaming 20 knots.

To reach a decisive conclusion most nations' cruisers, including those of Great Britain and Germany, carried torpedoes. If they hit, torpedoes punched holes in the hull below the waterline, which filled a ship with water, sinking it. However, torpedoes travelled only slightly faster than the targets at which they were aimed. Hitting an alert, manoeuvring cruiser with a torpedo was almost impossible.

Most battles between German and British heavy cruisers in World War II were fought in the war's opening years, between September 1939 and December 1942. (One was the next-to-last clash between Kriegsmarine and Royal Navy major surface units. It occurred on New Year's Eve in 1942. There were no others until 26 December 1943.)

If the Treaty of Versailles had yielded the results the victors intended, there should have been no German Navy capable of fielding ocean-raiding cruisers. The German

A peacetime photograph taken in the 1930s of HMS *Dorsetshire*, one of 13 County-class heavy cruisers built for the Royal Navy in the 1920s. The ship is dressed with flags for a celebration. Note the Fairey Seafox seaplane carried. (USNHHC)

Navy should have been a coastal defence force, operating in the Baltic. But the treaty's terms were ambiguous enough for the Reichsmarine, Germany's navy in the 1920s, to design *Panzerschiffe* intended for ocean raiding. Although the British called these 'pocket battleships', they were really cruisers with battleship guns.

Britain compounded this error by permitting Germany to build heavy cruisers and battleships in the late 1930s, a decision taken in hopes of counter-balancing the threat posed by the Soviet Union. Instead it created a viable Kriegsmarine (the 1935 heir to the Reichsmarine) to challenge the Royal Navy. It was a task the Kriegsmarine's officers and men eagerly accepted, in hopes of avenging German naval defeat in World War I.

The war's opening was a period where the heavy cruiser still reigned supreme in the open ocean. Battleships spent most of their time at port swinging at their moorings. Aircraft had not come to dominate the seas as they would later in the war. Fast-stepping cruisers proved elusive to U-boats and submarines. The British had to guard their sea lanes using a cruiser fleet that included 15 heavy cruisers. Germany wanted to strike at British shipping, and reluctant to use their battleships, risked their *Panzerschiffe* or heavy cruisers instead.

The crews of the cruisers that fought the Battle of the River Plate parade past Nelson's Column in London as part of victory celebrations held for the battle. They are marching to London's Guildhall to participate in a celebratory banquet. (AC)

Fight they did; not often, because Germany had few heavy cruisers and was reluctant to risk them unnecessarily. Nevertheless, German and British heavy cruisers clashed. In the South Atlantic, North Atlantic, the frigid waters of the Denmark Strait and the Arctic approaches to the Soviet Union, German and British cruisers fought each other. The battles, while rare, were noteworthy.

Fights between cruisers during World War II captured public fascination in the same way frigate duels had during the 18th and 19th centuries. It was the modern version of medieval trial by combat, where two evenly matched foes fought until a decision was reached. The public cheered over or groaned at the results of cruiser battles as if they were prize fights. Victors were feted and lauded. So were German captains who conducted successful Atlantic raids.

The consequences of defeat or victory could be the loss of a single ship, as with the battle in which *Admiral Graf Spee* was lost. It could also be far more. The outcome of one duel decided the fate of a convoy carrying troops, tanks and aircraft upon which the fortunes of a 1941 British offensive in North Africa hinged. The outcome of another led to the demobilization of the Kriegsmarine's surface fleet.

CHRONOLOGY

1915
9 June   Britain orders Hawkins-class cruisers, 10,000-ton 'light' cruisers intended to hunt down German raiders. They become the basis of all subsequent heavy cruiser designs.

1919
28 June   Germany signs the Treaty of Versailles ending World War I. Among other things, it sharply limits the size of the Reichsmarine, the German Navy.

1922
6 February   Washington Treaty signed, creating a 10-year ban on building battleships, but permitting construction of cruisers of up to 10,000 tons displacement and guns no larger than 8in.

2 November   Design of the Kent-class cruisers authorized.

1924
15 September   HMS *Berwick* is laid down.

1927
May   York-class cruisers are authorized.
8 July   HMS *Norfolk* is laid down.

1928
15 February   HMS *Berwick* completed.
23 February   HMS *Suffolk* completed.
1 August   HMS *Exeter* is laid down.

1930
22 April   First London Naval Treaty signed, creating a distinction between heavy cruisers (armed with 8in. guns) and light cruisers (armed with 6in. or smaller guns), and limiting heavy cruiser numbers.
30 April   HMS *Norfolk* completed.

1931
19 May   *Deutschland* launched.
23 July   HMS *Exeter* completed.

1932
1 October   *Admiral Graf Spee* is laid down.

1933
30 January   Adolf Hitler becomes Chancellor of Germany.

1935
16 March   Hitler abrogates the Treaty of Versailles.
1 June   Reichsmarine abolished and replaced by the Kriegsmarine.
18 June   Anglo-German Tonnage Agreement signed, permitting Germany to build its navy to 35 per cent the tonnage of the Royal Navy.

Admiral Hipper's first combat action was one of its most dramatic. It trapped the British destroyer HMS *Glowworm* alone and unsupported. This photo shows HMS *Glowworm*, unable to escape, crossing the bows of *Admiral Hipper* as HMS *Glowworm* turns to ram the German cruiser. (AC)

| 6 July | *Admiral Hipper* is laid down. |

1936
6 January	*Admiral Graf Spee* commissioned.
25 March	Second London Naval Treaty signed limiting cruisers to maximums of 8,000 tons displacement and 155mm guns.
23 April	*Prinz Eugen* is laid down.

1939
20 April	*Admiral Hipper* completed.
1 September	World War II begins.
13 December	Battle of the River Plate: HMS *Exeter*, HMS *Ajax* and HMNZS *Achilles* engage *Admiral Graf Spee* close to the Uruguayan coast.
17 December	*Admiral Graf Spee* scuttled.

1940
25 January	*Panzerschiff Deutschland* renamed *Lützow* and reclassified as a heavy cruiser.
1 August	*Prinz Eugen* is completed.
25 December	The Christmas Day Battle between *Admiral Hipper* and HMS *Berwick*.

1941
8 May	HMS *Cornwall* sinks the German auxiliary cruiser *Pinguin*.
24 May	Battle of the Denmark Strait: the heavy cruisers HMS *Norfolk* and HMS *Suffolk*, and *Prinz Eugen* all play an active role.
22 November	HMS *Devonshire* sinks German auxiliary cruiser *Atlantis*.
11 December	Germany and its allies declare war on the United States.

1942
| 1 March | HMS *Exeter* sunk by Japanese cruisers *Myoko* and *Ashigara* in the wake of the Battle of the Java Sea. |
| 2–5 July | Operation *Rösselsprung* takes place, an attempt to attack Convoy PQ 17 with Kriegsmarine surface ships. |

| 31 December | Battle of the Barents Sea: *Admiral Hipper* and *Lützow* fail to inflict significant losses on Convoy JW 51B. |

1945
2 May	*Admiral Hipper* scuttled by depth charges in Kiel harbour.
4 May	*Lützow* scuttled near Swinemünde in the Kaiserfahrt Kanal.
	War in Europe ends.
8 May	

1946
| 22 December | *Prinz Eugen* capsizes near Carlos Islet following its use in the Able and Baker atomic bomb tests at Bikini Atoll. |

1947
| 22 July | *Lützow* is refloated and then sunk in Danzig Bay. |

1948
| 25 March | HMS *Suffolk* sold for breaking up after being stricken from the Royal Navy. |
| 12 July | HMS *Berwick* sold for breaking up. |

1950
| 3 January | HMS *Norfolk* sold for breaking up. |

1958
| 3 November | HMS *Cumberland*, the last surviving Royal Navy heavy cruiser, is paid off. It is sold for scrapping and broken up in 1959. |

HMS *Sheffield* with HMS *Cornwall* behind it in 1939. In 1942, HMS *Sheffield*, a Town-class light cruiser, would successfully defeat Kriegsmarine heavy cruisers at the Battle of the Barents Sea, while County-class HMS *Cornwall* would be sunk by Japanese carrier aircraft off Ceylon. (AC)

DESIGN AND DEVELOPMENT

With the advent of steam, the wooden sailing frigate was replaced by a new class of warship: the cruiser. By the last decades of the 19th century, three types of steel-hulled, steam-powered cruisers emerged: the armoured cruiser, the protected cruiser and the light or scout cruiser.

Armoured cruisers were the largest, typically 10,000–14,000 tons. As large as battleships, they were faster, with less armour, and a main battery of 7.5in.–9.2in. guns. Protected cruisers had thinner armour, displaced 5,000–10,000 tons and typically carried 6in. main batteries. Their armour usually protected machinery and magazines. The light cruiser was unarmoured, displaced 3,000–5,000 tons and had main batteries of 4in.–5.5in. guns.

These ships fulfilled the roles traditionally performed by frigates: scouting for the fleet, commerce raiding and commerce protection. Whether a light, protected or armoured cruiser was used depended upon availability, and the potential threat. A squadron of armoured cruisers or protected cruisers might lead a battle fleet to scout out the enemy's battle line and drive off cruisers attempting to locate its own battle line. Light cruisers might be sent in a wide arc ahead of the fleet to fix the enemy's location.

The first two decades of the 20th century witnessed changes to the cruiser due to the appearance of torpedoes, the dreadnought battleship, radio and aircraft. Light cruisers gained a new role: leading flotillas of torpedo boats or torpedo boat destroyers. The armoured cruiser, which sacrificed speed for protection, became obsolescent due to the introduction of the dreadnought.

The biggest change was wrought by radio. Previously, communications were limited by the distance to the horizon. Wireless telegraphy allowed messages to be sent hundreds or thousands of miles. It allowed cruisers to scout well ahead of the fleet, radioing back contact reports. It also allowed information to be sent to commerce-protecting cruisers, allowing them to intercept commerce raiders or guard against them. This further increased the value of the fast light and protected cruisers.

By the time World War I began, all nations had abandoned the armoured cruiser in favour of the other two cruiser classes. The armoured cruiser's role was being filled by the battlecruiser, a large, fast dreadnought with battleship guns.

Radio – wireless telegraphy – led to the creation of the early 20th-century cruiser, a fast, lightly armoured and heavily armed warship. Radio allowed ships to be dispatched to problem spots quickly. These are the radio aerials between the masts of HMS *Cornwall*. (USNHHC)

Aircraft also changed the cruiser's role, although by how much was not apparent by 1920. World War I showed the aircraft could supplement or even replace the cruiser's scouting role. Aircraft armed with airborne torpedoes might even serve as a ship destroyer. The primitive aircraft of World War I were too fragile to pose a serious threat to large warships, including cruisers. The few ships sunk by aircraft during that war usually were exceptions.

Aircraft grew in capability, offering both increased threats and increased opportunity for cruisers. Even as aircraft grew powerful enough for dive-bombers and torpedo planes to threaten cruisers, they offered an expansion of the cruiser's capability. Aircraft carried aboard cruisers could expand a cruiser's scouting range, and provide gunnery spotting. Moreover, the emergence of aircraft offered cruisers new roles as an anti-aircraft platform or fighter director.

None of this was apparent when the heavy cruiser arrived on the scene. The heavy cruiser was a hybrid, blending the speed and size of protected cruisers with the guns of the armoured cruiser. The World War II heavy cruiser was the child of the 1922 Washington Naval Treaty. The treaty defined the heavy cruiser while simultaneously creating a demand for them. Germany and Great Britain built heavy cruisers within the constraints various naval limitations treaties placed, to accommodate their nations' perceived naval interests.

THE TREATY CRUISER

The heavy cruiser was born out of naval arms limitation treaties. The German heavy cruiser was also born of naval treaties, although it came into being through bilateral naval treaties between Britain and Germany.

11

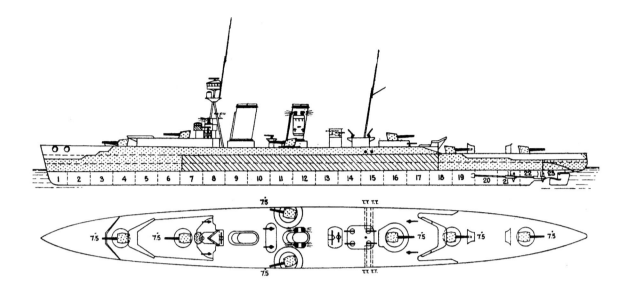

The Hawkins class comprised large, 10,000-ton cruisers designed to hunt down German raiders during World War I. Heavily armed, their existence was the main reason Britain wanted a 10,000-ton and 8in.-gun limit on the size of cruisers in the Washington Naval Treaty, even though they had no intention of building cruisers larger than 7,000 tons and carrying 6in. main guns. (AC)

As World War I ended, most navies were building relatively small cruisers – between 5,000 and 7,000 tons, armed with 4in. to 6in. guns, lightly armoured and fast. The US Omaha class (built between 1918 and 1924), British 'D' class (1916–22) and Japanese Sendai class (1922–25) all fit these parameters. While classified as light cruisers, they had some armour and would have been considered protected cruisers prior to World War I.

No one was building armoured cruisers, and no one planned cruisers with main guns larger than 6in. The 6,000-ton cruiser with mid-sized guns was viewed as the best design for the duties expected of cruisers. Britain experimented during World War I, building larger light cruisers: the Hawkins and 'E' classes. The former displaced 10,000 tons and carried 7.5in. main guns. The latter displaced 8,300 tons, with 6in. guns. They were wartime designs intended to run down German surface raiders.

By the time the Hawkins were completed, the German surface raiders were gone and the ships were white elephants. Only five were built. One was converted to an aircraft carrier while under construction. Similarly, only two 'E'-class cruisers were built, a response to rumoured, but non-existent, German 'supercruisers'. Both classes were viewed as too large and uneconomical, despite being among the newest British cruisers in 1922.

Following World War I, Japan, Great Britain and the United States became involved in a naval arms race. Italy and France began a similar race against each other. The ships in these competitions were dreadnoughts – battleships and battlecruisers. They were expensive. Britain and the US were mired in a post-war recession and Japan risked bankruptcy completing the ships outlined in its building programme.

In 1921, the US opened a conference to discuss naval disarmament in Washington DC. It was attended by the US, Great Britain, Japan, France and Italy. It led to the signing of the 1922 Washington Naval Treaty by these five powers. The treaty limited the total dreadnought tonnage each nation could possess, created a ten-year 'holiday' during which dreadnoughts could not be built and limited the size of future dreadnoughts to 35,000 tons displacement. Older warships were to be scrapped, and some dreadnoughts under construction were to be scrapped or converted to aircraft carriers to bring nations down to treaty limits.

The treaty set no limit on the total tonnage or number of cruisers each nation could build. However, to prevent nations from building dreadnought substitutes in the form of large 'cruisers', the treaty set limits on the displacement and largest guns which could be carried by cruisers. Under the terms of any treaty signed, ships in excess of the limits set would have to be scrapped.

The obvious limit was 7,000 tons and 6in. guns. In 1922, no nation planned cruisers larger than that. But Britain possessed six new cruisers, some still under construction, which exceeded those limits. Additionally, they were among the few British cruisers with a large operational range; the rest had been built to operate in the North Sea. The cruisers would have to be replaced by new construction, which in British eyes mitigated the cost savings gained by signing.

Instead, Britain negotiated a hike in cruiser limits. The Hawkins class displaced 10,000 tons and carried a main battery of 7.5in. guns. To allow Britain to keep them, the maximum allowable displacement was negotiated as 10,000 tons. The maximum main battery was negotiated as 8in. guns. This was larger than the Hawkins battery, but those were an unusual, one-off calibre. Most nations (including Britain) had 8in. guns, so that was the calibre set.

Except for Britain, no nation had ordered a cruiser displacing more than 7,000 tons or carrying a main battery of 8in. or larger since the end of the 1904–05 Russo-Japanese War. Before signing the 1922 Washington Naval Treaty, Britain had no intention of building more large cruisers. Then the law of unintended consequences kicked in.

Because the Washington Treaty permitted 10,000-ton cruisers with 8in. main guns while banning construction of battleships, the United States, Japan, Italy and France soon began ordering these types of cruisers, forcing Britain to follow suit or be outclassed. This is the Italian heavy cruiser *Zara*, laid down in 1929. (AC)

The 1922 Washington Naval Treaty failed to end the naval rivalry between Japan and the United States. Rather, it redirected this into cruisers. A 10,000-ton cruiser with an 8in. battery was a poor substitute for a dreadnought, but could overpower several of the then-conventional smaller 6in. cruisers. There were no limits on the number that could be built, only their maximum size. The US and Japan eagerly plunged into a race to build 8in. cruisers. Britain, France and Italy had to join it.

By 1930, dozens of cruisers displacing 10,000 tons with 8in. guns had been commissioned and were being constructed throughout the world. More were planned. The United States had a dozen in commission or actively under construction. Japan had eight (and four slightly smaller 8in. cruisers), France and Italy seven each. Britain was winning the cruiser race by 1930, with 14 built and one under construction, including two 8in. cruisers under treaty maximums.

It was not a race Britain sought, and by the end of the 1920s, Britain wished to see it ended. At the Geneva Naval Conference in 1927, Britain proposed a tonnage limit on 8in. cruisers similar to that on dreadnoughts, and limiting future construction to 7,500 tons per ship. The solution favoured Britain with its 15 new cruisers, but the United States planned more treaty cruisers. The proposal went nowhere.

Instead, a new agreement was hammered out at the 1930 London Naval Conference. The resultant London Naval Treaty set tonnage limits on 8in. cruisers, destroyers and submarines possessed by each signatory nation. It restricted future cruiser construction to a maximum displacement of 7,500 tons with a 6.1in. (155mm) main battery.

Finally, it created a new category of warship. Henceforth, the 8in. cruisers, previously classified as light cruisers, became heavy cruisers. It was signed by the same five powers that signed the Washington Naval Treaty. It ended the 8in. cruiser race. It also meant Britain's newest heavy cruisers would be nearly a decade old when World War II began.

BRITISH HEAVY CRUISERS

The signing of the Washington Naval Treaty fired the starting gun for the heavy cruiser race. Britain had the inside track. The Hawkins class left Britain the only navy with recent experience building a 10,000-ton, large-gun cruiser. Yet Britain was initially reluctant to build 10,000-ton 'treaty' cruisers. Reports the US and Japan were ordering treaty cruisers forced Britain's hand.

What became the heavy cruiser did fill an urgent strategic need for Britain. In 1922, Britain had 83 cruisers, more than any other nation's navy, including the United States. Moreover, all were of recent construction, almost all having been built since the start of World War I.

In 1922, Britain had the world's largest merchant fleet and colonies scattered around the globe. Commerce protection was one of the Royal Navy's most important responsibilities. Guarding Britain's sea lanes was a task for cruisers. Britain needed a large cruiser fleet. However, Britain had the wrong cruiser force for effective commerce protection. Except for the Hawkins- and 'E'-class ships, British cruisers were built for the North and Mediterranean seas, not oceans. Most had a range of fewer than 6,000 NM when cruising at 10kn; too short and too slow for patrolling Atlantic sea lanes, let alone those in the broader Pacific Ocean.

Existing, superannuated armoured cruisers filled this role during World War I, allowing Britain to concentrate its wartime cruiser construction on ships intended against the now non-existent German High Seas Fleet. These armoured cruisers were retired and scrapped after the peace treaty ending World War I was signed in 1919.

The 1930 treaty cruiser sounded like an excellent replacement. The Hawkins class demonstrated the range potential of a 10,000-ton cruiser. Bunker oil weight did not count against treaty weight limits, and empty fuel tanks weighed almost nothing (the weight of air in the tanks' volume). Voluminous fuel could be designed into the hull.

An 8in. main battery could deal with any potential surface commerce raider. Even if a navy wanted a battleship to serve as a lone commerce raider, other

The launch of HMS *Kent* on 16 March 1926. *Kent* was the lead ship of the 13-ship County-class cruisers built for the Royal Navy. Originally classed as light cruisers, they were retroactively re-rated heavy cruisers by the 1930 London Naval Treaty. (USNHHC)

nations' existing dreadnoughts lacked the range and speed to serve as one. The most powerful conceivable foe faced would be another treaty cruiser – evening the odds. Individual light cruisers or auxiliary cruisers were easy prey for an 8in. cruiser. (Auxiliary cruisers were warships converted from merchant ships, often fast liners, and frequently disguised as unarmed tramp steamers.)

The new cruisers needed to be fast enough to catch any fleeing raider. Disguised auxiliary cruisers rarely topped 20kn but existing light cruisers used for raiding could reach 28kn. A top speed of 33–35kn was desirable. Based on prior experience, a hull displacing 10,000 tons required a power plant capable of generating 100,000 hp to reach that.

Triple-gun turrets were considered for the main battery, but twin turrets were chosen: the triple turret was viewed as too complex. Designs for twin turrets existed; a triple turret would have to be designed, delaying construction. Using twin turrets yielded a main battery of eight guns in four turrets. With Nos. 2 and 3 turrets superfiring over Nos. 1 and 4, it permitted an eight-gun broadside, with four available in chases.

Three initial designs were submitted, mainly differing in armour arrangement. Two protected the magazines in a 4in.-armour citadel, but left the deck and sides over the

HMS *EXETER*

Displacement:	8,390 tons (normal), 10,660 tons (full load)
Dimensions:	575ft 1in. x 58ft x 17in.
Propulsion:	Four Parsons geared high-pressure steam turbine (four shafts), eight Admiralty three-drum boilers, 80,000 shp (designed)
Speed:	32kn
Range:	10,000 NM at 10kn
Fuel:	Oil
Crew:	628 officers, petty officers and sailors
Armament (1939):	Six 8in./50-calibre guns (3x2), four 4in./50-calibre guns (4x1), six 21in. torpedo tubes (2×3)
Aircraft:	Up to two Walrus seaplanes, two catapults
Armour:	Side: 3in. Deck: 1.5in. Magazine: 5.5in. Turret: 2in. (all max)

HMS *Exeter* was the final heavy cruiser built by the Royal Navy. It was slightly larger than its older, near-sister HMS *York* and can be distinguished from it by a lower conning tower superstructure and straight (rather than raked) funnels and masts.

Intended for service on remote stations where the main naval threat was individual surface raiders, *Exeter* spent much of its pre-war career assigned to the American and West Indies station. When World War II started, it was sent to the South Atlantic. In company with light cruisers HMS *Ajax* and HMNZS *Achilles*, it tracked down *Admiral Graf Spee*. The hunt ended with the Battle of the River Plate, in which HMS *Exeter* was badly damaged, and *Admiral Graf Spee* scuttled. These illustrations show HMS *Exeter* as it appeared at the Battle of the River Plate.

Following repairs, HMS *Exeter* was assigned to the Far East. It fought at the Battle of the Java Sea, where it was damaged, and sunk the following day by Japanese cruisers while attempting to escape to Australia.

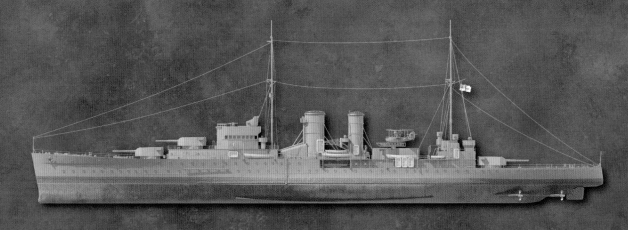

HMAS *Australia* was one of two Kent-class cruisers built for Australia. As with the rest of the County-class cruisers, it had a main battery of eight 8in. guns. (AC)

machinery spaces unprotected. The third design reduced magazine armour to 3in., but provided 2in. belt and 1in. deck armour over the machinery.

The Admiralty rejected all three. It wanted the magazines protected by 6in. armour, the minimum capable of stopping an 8in. shell at close ranges. It was willing to accept 4in. armour, but not less. Four inches would stop most fire from 6in. guns or smaller, and would stop an 8in. shell hitting at oblique angles. The Admiralty also wanted the machinery spaces protected.

The compromise reached was to reduce the machinery spaces, lowering the design's horsepower to 75,000 shp (shaft horsepower). Weight savings from the machinery reduction were applied to protection. Side magazine armour remained at 4in., with 3in. horizontal armour. The machinery spaces, shell-handing rooms and steering gained 1in. of vertical plating, with the shell-handling rooms receiving 1in. and the machinery spaces 1½in. of horizontal protection.

In addition to 8in. guns, the cruiser design included torpedoes, equipping it with two quadruple-mount torpedo tubes on each broadside firing conventional 21in. torpedoes. They were mounted amidships on the weather deck. This torpedo was still under design when the first of these cruisers were being developed, but the Admiralty wished to include them. The area allocated to the torpedo mounting included enough extra space to permit replacement with the 24½in. oxygen torpedoes during a future refit.

The cruiser's secondary battery consisted of four single-mount, high-altitude 4in. guns. These were intended as anti-aircraft as well as anti-surface ship guns. Provisions were made to mount two quadruple pompoms, two quadruple 0.5in. machine guns or four single pompoms. This cruiser was one of the first designs to

HMS *BERWICK*

Displacement:	9,750 tons (normal), 13,450 tons (full load)
Dimensions:	630ft x 68ft 5in. x 16ft 3in.
Propulsion:	Four Brown Curtis geared high-pressure steam turbines (four shafts), eight Admiralty three-drum boilers, 80,000 shp (designed)
Speed:	32.34kn (at trials)
Fuel:	Fuel oil
Range:	13,300 NM at 12kn
Crew:	784 officers, petty officers and sailors
Armament (1938):	Eight 8in./50-calibre guns (4x2), four 4in./50-calibre guns (4x1), 16 2pdr pom-poms (2x8), eight 21in. torpedo tubes (2×4)
Aircraft:	Up to three Walrus seaplanes, two catapults
Armour:	Belt: 4in. Deck: 1.5in. Magazine: 3in. Turret: 1in. (all max)

HMS *Berwick* was the second of five Kent-class cruisers built for the Royal Navy. Following commissioning, it was sent to the China Station, where it remained until 1936. It was then assigned to the Mediterranean during the Abyssinian Crisis. It underwent a refit in 1937–38, where the belt armour protecting the machinery spaces was increased to 4.5in., twin 4in. AA replaced the original single 4in. guns and eight barrelled pompoms replaced quad pompoms.

HMS *Berwick* spent World War II in European waters, participating in the Norwegian campaign, the British occupation of Iceland and the Battle of Cape Spartivento, prior to engaging *Admiral Hipper* on Christmas Day 1940. This plate depicts *Berwick* at the Christmas Day Battle.

HMS *Berwick* served in the Home Fleet for the rest of the war, escorting Arctic convoys. In October 1944, it carried Free Norwegian forces to Murmansk so they could help liberate Finnmark.

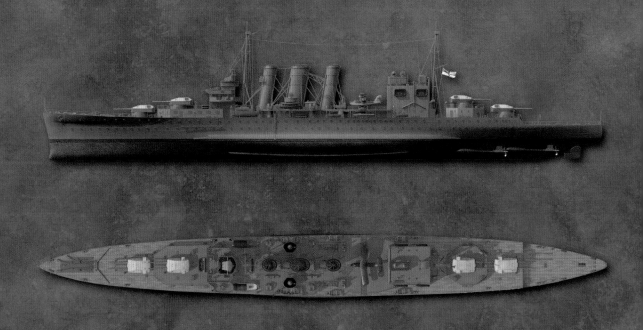

include anti-aircraft batteries during the design stage. For the 1920s, the battery was powerful.

The cruiser also had provision to carry three aircraft, including a centreline hangar and a catapult mounted on each side amidships to launch aircraft. The aircraft were floatplanes, intended to land on water and be hoisted back aboard by cranes.

Everything had to fit within 10,000 tons, requiring weight reductions. Some weight reduction was achieved through legerdemain. The ships' magazines had space for 150 shells, but they carried only 100 during peacetime, cutting 50 tons from the design displacement. More weight was saved by reducing the ships' boats carried. The resulting design limited growth capabilities. Adding anti-aircraft guns or as-yet uninvented radar and radio direction-finding equipment (and dynamos to power them) without removing something topside would leave these ships dangerously top heavy, but this all lay in the future.

The resulting County-class cruisers (named for British counties) became the first treaty cruisers built. The first set, the Kent class, displaced 10,000 tons, had a maximum speed of 32kn and could cruise, without refuelling, for 13,300 NM at 12kn. Britain ordered 17 Kent-class cruisers, but cut that order to five for budgetary reasons: HMSs *Kent, Berwick, Suffolk, Cumberland* and *Cornwall*. Two more, HMASs *Australia* and *Canberra*, were added after Australia agreed to buy and run them. All seven were completed by mid-1928. A further six were ordered later: four London-class cruisers (HMSs *London, Sussex, Shropshire* and *Devonshire*), and two Dorsetshire-class cruisers (HMSs *Dorsetshire* and *Norfolk*). These classes included minor modifications, but adhered to the basic Kent design. They were completed by 1931.

Britain built two more heavy cruisers before the London Treaty halted construction of the type. These were HMSs *York* and *Exeter*, the product of budget limitations and

HMS *Exeter* was the second of two York-class heavy cruisers the Royal Navy ordered, and the last heavy cruiser built by Britain. Its main battery comprised six 8in. guns. (AC)

the need for more cruisers. Smaller than the County class, they displaced 8,200 tons and carried only six 8in. guns in three twin turrets. They were downscaled in other ways: they had six torpedo tubes instead of eight, one aircraft and no hangar. They maintained the same anti-aircraft suite as the Counties, however.

These ships were intended for commerce protection on remote stations, such as in the South Atlantic or Indian oceans, where they would be unlikely to encounter enemy heavy cruisers, but likely to come across disguised raiders. They, too, had a 12,000 NM range at a speed of 14kn and a 32kn top speed. HMS *Exeter* was the last heavy cruiser built for the Royal Navy. After that, Britain stuck to light cruisers. That meant when Britain did face German heavy cruisers during World War II, it would be fighting with ships designed 15 years earlier, against ships started only a few years before 1939.

GERMAN *PANZERSCHIFFE*

Germany and the Soviet Union were the only industrialized nations that did not participate in the heavy cruiser race triggered by the Washington Naval Treaty. In the 1920s, the Soviets were too riven by internal strife to be interested in building warships. Germany was barred from building them by treaty.

The Treaty of Versailles, formally ending World War I, and signed by Germany in 1919, limited the size of the Reichsmarine, following the abdication of Kaiser Wilhelm and introduction of a German republic. The treaty intended to prevent Germany from becoming a future threat to the Allied powers. The Reichsmarine was permitted only six battleships, six cruisers and 24 destroyers and torpedo boats. No U-boats were permitted. The limits set intended to permit a German navy to counter-balance the Soviets in the Baltic, while ensuring German ships were incapable of operating in the Atlantic.

The *Admiral Scheer*, the second of the three Deutschland-class *Panzerschiffe*. These ships were revolutionary in many ways. They were cruisers carrying battleship guns, and the first extensively welded, diesel-powered capital ships ever built. (AC)

Germany was only permitted to keep pre-dreadnought battleships, and allowed cruisers with guns no larger than 155mm. No warship could be replaced until it was 20 years old, and the maximum displacement of ships replacing the pre-dreadnought battleships was limited to 10,000 tons (smaller than the displacement of Germany's existing pre-dreadnoughts). While no limit was placed on the size of the guns these

replacements could mount, the Allies believed any guns bigger than 280mm (11in.) on a ship of 10,000 tons displacement would sacrifice too much in protection and stability.

The oldest of the German battleships turned 20 years old in 1924. The Reichsmarine began planning replacements that year. The resulting design met the conditions set by the Treaty of Versailles while evading the intentions behind the conditions. It was a long-range warship capable of serving as an independent Atlantic commerce raider.

The ship was the *Deutschland*. While it replaced a battleship, it was to all intents an armoured cruiser. It was a throwback to the original battlecruisers, the Japanese Tsukuba-class cruisers. These ships were labelled armoured cruisers, but substituted battleship 12in. turrets for the original 8in. guns during construction.

Similarly, *Deutschland* and its sisters (*Admiral Graf Spee* and *Admiral Scheer*) mounted battleship-sized 280mm guns in two triple turrets. Like battleships (and armoured cruisers), they had a secondary battery of eight 150mm guns and a tertiary battery of 88mm anti-aircraft guns (six, in three twin turrets). They also carried eight 533mm (21in.) torpedoes in two quad mounts aft of the stern turret. However, unlike the 18kn battleships they replaced, they could reach a speed of 28kn.

They could travel 10,000 NM at 20kn, a phenomenal range. To achieve that range while staying within the 10,000-ton displacement limit, these ships were propelled by diesels, the first major warships to use diesels rather than steam plants. They had eight MAN 7,100 bhp diesels, with four motors on each shaft. When cruising, only one diesel was used on each shaft.

Germany did not classify these ships as battleships or cruisers. The former term was avoided because these ships were far more fragile than battleships. Germany did not want potential opponents to gain the prestige of sinking a German 'battleship' if the *Deutschland* or its sisters went down. Since the Versailles treaty banned construction of 10,000-ton cruisers, the Reichsmarine used the ambiguous term *Panzerschiff* (armoured ship). The British, seeking to amplify their menace, dubbed them 'pocket battleships'.

These ships were far from battleships. Belt armour was 130mm (5.1in.) maximum, tapering to 18mm at the bow and 30mm at the stern. The turrets had armour up to 170mm thick. This was substantially heavier than a treaty cruiser, but similar to armour carried by the post-treaty Baltimore-class heavy cruisers the US Navy built during World War II. The Deutschlands only technically adhered to the 10,000-ton displacement limit. While the official displacement was listed as 10,800 tons, standard displacement was actually 12,400 tons. The ships were all-welded to reduce weight.

The design took a long time to finalize, and construction started on the first, RMS *Deutschland*, in February 1929. The ship was launched in May 1931 and entered service on 1 April 1933. *Deutschland* was joined in 1935 by *Admiral Scheer* and in 1936 by *Admiral Graf Spee*. They were more powerful than any cruiser then in commission and faster than any dreadnought, except for a few battlecruisers.

As *Admiral Scheer* joined the German fleet, Germany abrogated the Versailles treaty. Following this, Germany negotiated a bilateral treaty with Britain, allowing it to build a fleet to a tonnage up to 35 per cent of the Royal Navy's in all categories, including heavy cruisers.

The Reichsmarine began designing heavy cruisers in 1934, despite at that point being forbidden to build any. Their design then conformed to the 10,000 tons of the treaty limit. Once the Versailles treaty was dead, and the treaty with London negotiated, German ambitions grew bigger. The Germans, having signed no supplementary treaties, were permitted to build cruisers larger than 10,000 tons. While Britain wished to keep new cruiser construction under 7,500 tons, Britain agreed to permit Germany to build two larger cruisers under extraordinary circumstances. Those reasons were found when the Soviet Union began work on Kirov-class cruisers, mounting 180mm main guns.

The result was the Admiral Hipper class of heavy cruisers. Their nominal standard displacement was initially reported as 12,000 tons. In reality, standard displacement was closer to 16,000 tons, 60 per cent larger than Britain's heavy cruisers. They were larger and heavier than the Deutschland-class ships.

Much of that extra weight went into protection. Each had 80mm belt armour running from just ahead of the lead turret to just aft of the stern turret. Forward of it was a 40mm belt, and aft, protecting the steering gear, the armour was 70mm thick. Deck armour consisted of two layers, which combined offered 65mm of armour over the middle of the ship tapering to 12mm at the bow and stern. The turrets were encased by up to 105mm of steel.

These ships were heavily armed. They carried a main battery of eight 203mm guns in four twin turrets, a secondary armament of 12 twin-mounted dual-purpose 105mm guns and an anti-aircraft battery of 12 37mm and eight single-mount 20mm guns. They carried 12 torpedo tubes, six on each side in triple-tube mountings. They also had a catapult and could carry up to three floatplanes – Arado Ar 196s during World War II.

They could reach 32kn, but were short-legged ships. They could only travel 6,700 NM at a cruising speed of 17kn. They had three Blohm & Voss steam turbines generating 132,000 shp fed by 12 high-pressure boilers. The power plant drank up fuel.

The Admiral Hipper heavy cruisers deliberately flouted several limitations imposed by the naval treaties. They violated the abrogated Treaty of Versailles, but they also ignored the Washington Naval Treaty's 10,000-ton limit on cruiser designs. They displaced 15,600 tons light and 18,208 tons fully loaded. (AC)

KMS *LÜTZOW*

Displacement:	12,430 tons (normal), 14,290 tons (full load)
Dimensions:	186m (610ft 3in.) x 21.69m (71ft 2in.) x 7.25m (23ft 9in.)
Propulsion:	Eight MAN nine-cylinder Diesel (two shafts), 48,390 shp (designed)
Speed:	28kn
Fuel:	Diesel oil
Range:	13,300 NM at 12kn
Crew:	30 officers and 1,040 men
Armament (1942):	Six 290mm/52-calibre guns (2x3), eight 150mm/55-calibre guns (8x1), six 105mm/65-calibre anti-aircraft guns (6x1), eight 37mm Flak (8x1), eight 20mm Flak (8x1), eight 21in. torpedo tubes (2×4)
Aircraft:	Two Arado Ar 196, one catapult
Armour:	Belt: 130mm. Deck: 45mm. Turret: 170mm (all max)

Lützow was launched as *Deutschland*, but was renamed *Lützow* and reclassified as a heavy cruiser in January 1940. Officially this was to confuse enemy intelligence; the original *Lützow* was sold to the Soviets in February. More likely it was because Hitler did not want to risk losing a ship named *Deutschland*.

As *Deutschland*, it participated in goodwill cruises in 1934–35 and 1938–39. During the Spanish Civil War in 1936–37, it was sent to the Spanish coast, conducting non-intervention patrols. It conducted a commerce raiding cruise between September and November 1939, sinking or capturing only three ships.

As *Lützow*, it participated in the 1940 invasion of Norway, where it was damaged in the same action in which *Blücher* was sunk. Following repairs, it served in Norwegian or Baltic waters for the rest of the war. It participated in the Battle of the Barents Sea with *Admiral Hipper*, fleeing from two British light cruisers. These illustrations show *Lützow* as it appeared before the battle.

Launching ceremonies for KMS *Seydlitz*. The fifth Hipper-Class heavy cruiser ordered by the Kriegsmarine, it was launched but never completed. After launch, work began to convert *Seydlitz* into a light aircraft carrier, but the conversion was abandoned after 1943. (AC)

Admiral Hipper was the first of these ships to be started and completed. It was laid down in July 1935 and commissioned in April 1939. It was followed by *Blücher* and *Prinz Eugen*, which were laid down in 1936 and commissioned in 1939 and 1940 respectively. Two other ships were started: *Seydlitz* in 1936 and *Lützow* in 1937. Both were launched before World War II began, but neither was completed. *Lützow* was sold to the Soviet Union incomplete in February 1940, while work stopped on *Seydlitz* in summer 1940. The latter was scuttled at the war's end.

When World War II began, Germany had four commissioned warships that were effectively heavy cruisers: the three Deutschlands and *Admiral Hipper*. The number would rise briefly to five with the addition of *Blücher* on 20 September 1939 before falling back to four due to war losses. It hovered between three and four for the rest of the war. Against them were ranged 15 British heavy cruisers, none of which individually matched their German counterparts.

KMS *ADMIRAL HIPPER*

Displacement:	15,600 tons (normal), 18,208 tons (full load)
Dimensions:	202.8m (665ft 4in.) x 21.3m (69ft 11in.) x 7.2m (24ft)
Propulsion:	Three Blohm & Voss high-pressure single-reduction geared steam turbines (three shafts), 12 × 80kg/cm La Mont boilers, 133,631 shp (designed)
Speed:	32.5kn
Fuel:	Fuel oil
Range:	6,500 NM at 17kn
Crew:	42 officers and 1,340 men
Armament (1940):	Eight 203mm/60-calibre guns (4x2), 12 105mm/65-calibre guns (6x2), 12 37mm Flak (6x2), two 20mm Flak (2x1), 12 21in. (533mm) torpedo tubes (4×3)
Aircraft:	Three Arado Ar 196, one catapult
Armour:	Belt: 80mm. Deck: 50mm. Turret: 105mm (all max)

The name ship of its class, *Admiral Hipper* entered service four months before World War II started. Still going through trials at the outset, it patrolled the Baltic before returning to the dockyard for modifications.

During the April 1940 invasion of Norway, the flagship of the force was sent to capture Trondheim. While successful, it was damaged after being rammed by the British destroyer HMS *Glowworm*. *Admiral Hipper* conducted two raids in the Atlantic, from November to December 1940 (where it fought HMS *Berwick*) and February 1941, sinking eight or nine merchant ships. It returned to Germany after the second.

Admiral Hipper went after Convoy PQ 17 in July 1942, but was recalled. It participated in the hunt for Convoy JW 51, culminating in the Battle of the Barents Sea. Damaged during the battle, it was decommissioned. Further damaged undergoing repairs, the wreck was scuttled in Kiel on 3 May 1945.

This plate depicts *Admiral Hipper* as it appeared at the 1940 Christmas Day Battle.

THE STRATEGIC SITUATION

World War II was the child of World War I. Its origins are complex and go beyond the explanation 'Germany started it' widely accepted in the decades that followed. Nationalist movements and territorial ambitions of Austria–Hungary, Russia and France contributed. So did economic rivalries between Europe's two biggest economies (and trading partners): Great Britain and Germany. After the war ended, the blame was heaped on Germany. Austria–Hungary and the Ottoman Empire had disintegrated. Imperial Russia was in the throes of a civil war leading to the rise of the Soviet Union. Only Germany remained, and the victorious Western Powers – France, Britain, Italy and the United States – were determined to make Germany pay for the war.

Negotiated in Paris between January and June 1919, the Treaty of Versailles ended World War I. It was signed on 28 June 1919. It stripped Germany of its colonial possessions, made Germany forfeit territories on its eastern and western frontiers and made it pay a massive indemnity to the victors. Germany was forbidden an air force. Its navy was reduced to performing coastal defence, and its army cut to a police force. The Rhineland, the province adjacent to France, was demilitarized, and France asserted the right to occupy the Ruhr, Germany's industrial heartland, if Germany defaulted on reparation payments.

Germans deeply resented Versailles, although Imperial Germany had imposed an equally harsh peace on France after the Franco-Prussian War of 1870–71 and Russia at the Treaty of Brest-Litovsk in March 1918. If Germany had defeated France in 1918, it planned to impose punitive peace terms. Regardless, the result was a festering resentment by Germans exceeding the festering resentment of the French after the Franco-Prussian War.

The Treaty of Versailles, negotiations for which are shown here, was intended to keep Germany too weak to ever threaten Britain and France again while keeping it strong enough to serve to check the Soviet Union. These self-contradictory goals left Germany angry and yet still able to retaliate against the victors of World War I. (AC)

Yet the Western Powers feared weakening Germany too much. Russia, convulsed by revolution, emerged with a communist government feared by the West. The Union of Soviet Socialist Republics promised equality of outcome. It instead delivered terror and dictatorship, wrapped in idealistic expansionism. If you were not interested in the revolution, the revolution was still interested in you. The victors kept post-World War I Germany largely intact. They did not force it to dissolve into the 19th-century collection of independent nations Prussia forged into Deutschland. Germany remained the largest and most populous nation in Continental Europe outside of Russia, and the most industrialized with the biggest economy. Moreover, the German people were resentful of what they viewed as an unjust peace.

To isolate the Soviet Union from Western Europe, the Treaty of Versailles created a wall of buffer states. By themselves they were too weak to contain the Soviets. France and Britain wanted to avoid military entanglements in Eastern Europe. They preferred a Germany powerful enough to counter-balance the Soviets, but too weak to threaten the victors. They desired a German Navy that could dominate the Baltic, and a German Army capable of stopping a thrust from Russia.

Meanwhile, the victorious powers were disarming. The armies, especially those of the English-speaking nations, were demobilized with small peacetime establishments retained. In 1919, Britain implemented the 'Ten Year Rule' for budgeting: the armed forces should assume Britain would not engage in a major war for ten years. The rule was renewed annually until 1932.

Britain, the United States and Japan continued building their navies, while France and Italy renewed building programmes interrupted by World War I. The pace threatened financial ruin, but no nation would stop if its rivals continued building. On 12 November 1921, the United States invited the other four nations to a conference discussing naval disarmament. By February 1922, agreement was reached limiting the size of each nation's navy, and the maximum displacement and battery carried by specific categories of ships and a pause in battleship construction. Germany was not invited to take part.

Germany soon waged a covert war against the Treaty of Versailles. It developed forbidden weapons systems, sometimes in cooperation with the Soviet Union which

The Deutschland-class *Panzerschiffe* were Germany's effort to sidestep the intention of the Treaty of Versailles while complying with the technicalities of the treaty. They were long-range cruisers instead of the coastal defence ships the treaty wanted the Germans to build. (AC)

the World War I victorious powers had hoped Germany would counter-balance. German workers, supported by the German government, went on a general strike in the French-occupied Ruhr.

Germany borrowed to finance the war, planning to pay off loans from collected indemnities after victory. Having lost, Germany had to pay back both loans and treaty-imposed indemnities. The debt load triggered hyperinflation in 1923, destroying the German economy and erasing personal savings. Unemployment and insolvency followed. The German economy had begun to recover by 1929. Then, a stock market crash in the United States triggered a global depression that lingered through much of the 1930s. Germany's rickety economy collapsed a second time, again leading to widespread unemployment.

Europe's victors were not much better off. World War I was fought over France's industrial belt, devastating it. France lost a staggering amount of manpower. Britain's industries were largely untouched, but fielding a large army for the first time, it too suffered tremendous casualties, especially among Britain's future leadership. The British Empire was overextended, a financial drain when Britain had little spare capital. Italy experienced massive losses during the war, and economic collapse and runaway inflation afterwards.

Budgetary worries led Britain to call a new naval limitations conference in London in 1930. Warships were expensive. The Washington Naval Treaty triggered a race to build large cruisers. The London Naval Treaty, signed in 1930, limited cruisers to a 7,500-ton displacement with guns no larger than 155mm (6.1in.), destroyers to a 1,850-ton displacement and a 130mm (5.1in.) gun limit and submarines to a 2,000-ton maximum. Exceptions were created for existing vessels, and a total tonnage limit was placed on each category of warship a nation could maintain.

The collapse of the pre-war economic systems led electorates to seek relief via totalitarian socialism. Communism was dominated by the Soviets. Nationalist versions of socialism – fascism – emerged in the 1920s. Fascism merged communism's features with racial identity. A paternalistic state was to be run for the benefit of the masses, but unlike communism only the masses belonging to the nation's ethnic majority benefitted. As in the Soviet Union, obedience to the state was a central tenet.

Italy was the first to fall under the sway of fascism. Benito Mussolini, a pre-war socialist, created the prototype Fascist party, gaining a political majority in Italy's parliament in 1924. A year later, he usurped power, leading to rule by the Fascist party. In Germany, Adolf Hitler's National Socialist German Workers (or Nazi) Party followed the same course. Hitler was elected chancellor of Germany's Reichstag in 1933. In 1934, he took power, making himself Germany's Führer (leader), suspending elections and making the Nazis Germany's ruling party.

Fascists kept power because fascism was widely popular, summarised by the maxim that it 'made the trains run on time'. Fascism seemed to deliver communism's promises – full employment and a government providing for the needs of its citizens – without nationalization of all property or official insistence on atheism. It offered prosperity and easy answers. Like communism, fascism insisted its subjects accept those answers without dissent. To explain problems, unpopular minorities were scapegoated; kulaks in the Soviet Union, Jews in Germany.

Like communism, fascism was expansionist. It viewed economics as a zero-sum game. For someone to gain, someone had to lose. Growth came at the expense of neighbouring powers. Italy under Mussolini and Germany under Hitler became aggressively expansionist.

France and Britain did not initially realize fascist expansionism, like communist expansionism, would continue until it was stopped, especially since Italy and Germany wrapped their demands with an initial veneer of reasonableness.

In March 1935, a year after declaring himself Führer, Hitler abrogated the Versailles treaty, rejecting its limitations on German military build-up and refusing further reparations payments. A few days earlier, he created a German Air Force, the Luftwaffe, forbidden by Versailles. France and Britain were unwilling to enforce the treaty, so Hitler's decisions stood. On 1 June 1935, Hitler replaced the Reichsmarine with the Kriegsmarine. A few days after establishing the latter, a bilateral naval treaty was signed with Britain. Britain agreed to let Germany build its navy to a tonnage 35 per cent of the Royal Navy's, including submarines. Almost immediately afterwards, Germany began a massive shipbuilding programme.

In 1936, Britain hosted another naval limitations conference. The United States, Britain and France attended. Italy and Japan, which would become Germany's Axis partners a few years later, did not. The resultant treaty extended the limits set in the 1930 London Naval Treaty until 1942, but quickly became a dead letter.

In 1936, Italy invaded Ethiopia. The Spanish Civil War began; pitting a constitutional republic against a fascist uprising. Germany remilitarized the Rhineland. Afterwards, it was learned that had the French sent in a dozen police into the Rhineland, the German Army would have retreated. The French did not, and Hitler was

Fearing the Soviets more than a re-armed Germany, Britain turned a blind eye to German naval rearmament, while facilitating Nazi territorial aggrandizement. Here, British Prime Minister Neville Chamberlain is congratulated after returning from Munich with a treaty granting Nazi Germany Czechoslovakia's Sudetenland in exchange for 'peace in our time'. (AC)

The 'peace in our time' British Prime Minister Neville Chamberlain negotiated at Munich on 30 September 1938 lasted less than a year. On 1 September 1939, the German battleship SMS *Schleswig-Holstein* opened World War II by bombarding Poland's Westerplatte military depot at Danzig. (AC)

emboldened. So was Italy, when its conquest of Ethiopia was challenged only by stiff diplomatic protests.

The slide towards war accelerated in 1938. Germany annexed Austria in March and the Sudetenland in September. The Sudetenland annexation was negotiated through the Munich Agreement. Britain, France and Italy agreed to permit Germany's taking of the strip of ethnic-German Czechoslovakia bordering Germany in exchange for Hitler's pledge that it would be his last territorial claim in Europe.

Britain began re-arming in 1938, but building large warships takes years. One year of peace remained. Britain had 15 heavy cruisers and 23 new 6in. gun-armed cruisers as 1939 started. Meanwhile, in March 1939, Germany declared a protectorate over the western Czech provinces of Moravia and Bohemia, and annexed Memel from Lithuania.

To stop German expansion, Britain and France guaranteed Poland's sovereignty. Hitler believed it a bluff and negotiated an alliance with the Soviet Union, dividing Poland between them. When Germany invaded Poland, Britain and France declared war on Germany.

When the war began, Britain had 35 cruisers built under the Washington Naval Treaty, three Hawkins-class and 24 older light cruisers, for a total of 62 cruisers. Britain would add another 19 to its fleet prior to the start of 1943, all of them light cruisers. Against that, Germany could field only four heavy cruisers (including the soon to be reclassified *Panzerschiffe*) capable of serving as Atlantic raiders. It would add only two more.

Based on numbers, the naval odds facing Germany seemed insurmountable. But Britain had to protect a worldwide trade network with its 62 cruisers. It also had to guard against the potential threat posed by Japan. Additionally, after France fell and Italy joined as an active belligerent, Britain had the Italian cruisers to combat – and potentially the French.

The British cruisers would be widely scattered. It was unlikely a lone German raider would have to deal with more than one British cruiser. In a one-on-one fight, the German cruiser had the material edge.

TECHNICAL SPECIFICATIONS

Any ship is a compromise between the desired displacement, protection, armament, speed and range. A ship designed under treaty restrictions has constraints on one or more of these elements. As we have seen, the Versailles treaty and Washington Naval Treaty limited displacement and armament. These limitations affected design, particularly affecting decisions relating to structure, propulsion and armament. Because the treaties limited weight, they affected soft elements critical to a ship's fighting efficiency, especially sensor electronics, like newly emerging radar.

STRUCTURE

The treaty cruisers (including German *Panzerschiffe*, built to Versailles weight limitations) represented a delicate balance between weight, hull strength and protection. The hull needed to be strong enough to stand up to North Atlantic winter storms, yet light enough to remain within the 10,000-ton limit set by treaty. Ships needed a high length-to-beam ratio for high speed (10:1 was desirable) but a long, thin hull made structural integrity challenging. Protection was a similar challenge. Thick armour offered safety, but armour plate was the densest material on a ship. Weight put into the hull structure deducted from weight available for machinery, guns and aircraft.

Laying the keel plates for HMS *Devonshire* in 1926. A heavy cruiser's hull and structure always represented a design compromise between the strength desired for the hull and the maximum weight permitted by treaty. (USNHHC)

Both County-class and York-class cruisers used riveted hulls (requiring plates to overlap), increasing weight. Britain did not use all-welded cruiser hull construction until the 1930s. Britain drew on its experience with large cruiser design, especially the Hawkins class, in developing hull structure. Framing was spaced to minimize weight while maximizing strength, as was plate thickness.

Armour was trickier. It was impossible to protect all critical spaces with a thickness of armour capable of resisting 8in. shells. Instead, emphasis was placed on protecting the ship's magazines. The goal was to prevent one lucky shot from sinking a cruiser by exploding the magazine. The magazines were shielded by up to 4.25in. of armour plate, enough to stop most 6in. shell hits, and 8in. shells which hit at an oblique angle. While the side armour and horizontal armour protecting the machinery spaces was only 1in. and 1½in. respectively (main turrets were similarly armoured), side armour was increased to 4in. during the last pre-war refits.

The Germans saved weight by welding hulls. *Deutschland* was one of the first welded cruiser-sized ships built (there was some rivetting). They also cheated, underreporting the weight of their ships. The Hippers particularly ignored treaty restrictions. Both designs yielded strong hulls, which proved good sea boats.

Both Deutschlands and Hippers had heavier armour than British treaty cruisers. In the Deutschlands, this was due to their smaller engines (48,390 hp to the Hippers' 133,000 hp and British cruisers' 80,000 hp) and because they had only two turrets. The weight saved permitted heavier armour elsewhere. With the Hippers, heavier armour resulted from ignoring treaty weight limits. Forty-two per cent of the Deutschland-class cruisers' weight and 15 per cent of the Admiral Hipper-class cruisers' went into armour as opposed to 11 per cent of the weight of a County-class cruiser. Despite that, the armour thicknesses on both classes of German cruisers were equivalent to the armour carried on the post-treaty US Baltimore-class heavy cruisers.

PROPULSION

Cruisers depended on speed, to reach a battle, catch a fleeing foe and run to safety when outmatched. By the 20th century, speed was a function of the power plant: how much horsepower the engines could send to the shafts, and how much of that horsepower the propeller could convert to thrust. *Panzerschiffe* were powered by diesel motors; British cruisers and the Hippers by high-pressure steam turbines.

The diesel was an internal combustion engine developed in Germany. By the 1930s, Germany produced the world's best diesels. A piston compressed an air–fuel mixture in a cylinder until it spontaneously combusted. The piston was driven by a crankshaft powered by the detonation of another cylinder in the motor.

Diesels were not as mechanically efficient as steam turbines, but they could start in minutes, not the hours required for an oil-fired boiler. A ship could cruise on one or

British heavy cruisers and the German Hipper-class heavy cruisers all used steam propulsion. These used boilers to superheat steam to drive steam turbines. In this picture, Royal Navy engineers take the temperature of the boiler furnace in a large warship. (AC)

two of its diesel motors (the Deutschlands had eight), with the others shut down. It typically took a quarter of a ship's maximum power to reach two-thirds of its top speed. With two motors running, Deutschlands could cruise at 20kn, allowing a long operational range with low fuel consumption.

The steam turbine was invented in Britain, and British steam power plants were among the world's best in the 1920s and 1930s. All British heavy cruisers had eight Admiralty-style three-drum boilers, each of which could generate 10,000 hp. Developed between the two world wars, these boilers produced 300 psi steam at 600 °F. External combustion engines, they were heated by fuel–oil-fired furnaces. The steam-powered Parsons steam turbines drove four propellers using gearing. It was a reliable power plant. The machinery displaced 1,850 tons. The turbines were fuel efficient, burning 2.9 tons of oil every hour steaming at 12kn.

The Hippers also used steam propulsion. It was the only way to get the desired power into the available space and weight. The first two used 12 La Mont boilers, each producing over 11,000 hp. They had a maximum steam pressure of 80kg/cm^2 (1,140 psi) at 842 °F. They were connected to three Blohm & Voss three-stage turbines. They drove three shafts. *Prinz Eugen* was equipped with Wagner boilers (80.7kg/cm^2 (1,029 psi) at 842 °F) and three-stage turbines. While this setup provided higher

Inside a German naval gun factory, workers put the final touches to naval artillery. This photo was probably taken before World War II began. (AC)

efficiency and more power, they also consumed fuel faster than the British steam plants. They were also less reliable due to their added complexity.

WEAPONRY

The main battery of a heavy cruiser was its principle weapon, the weapon around which it was designed. British heavy cruisers carried 8in. main batteries. German ships had either 280mm (11in.) or 203mm (8in.) main batteries.

British cruisers mounted Mark VIII breech-loading 8in. guns. These guns entered service in 1927, and were designed for treaty cruisers. They were 50-calibre guns (the barrel being 50 times longer than the bore), rifled with one turn in 30 calibres. The shells weighed 256lb, and had a separate powder charge. The maximum rate of fire was six rounds per minute and maximum range was 29,200yd (14.5 NM).

German *Panzerschiffe* mounted the 283mm SK (*Schnelladekanone* – quick-loading cannon) C/28. These were 52-calibre guns introduced in 1928. Shells weighed 300kg (661lb) and had separate powder charges. Their maximum rate of fire was two rounds per minute and their maximum range was 36,500m (19.7 NM). The Hipper-class cruisers carried SK C/34 203mm guns. These were first used on *Admiral Hipper*, entering service in 1939. They were 60-calibre guns, firing a 122kg (269lb) shell with separate charges. The maximum rate of fire was five rounds per minute; their maximum range was 33,500m (18.1 NM). Deutschland-class ships carried a secondary battery of 150mm, 55-calibre, breech-loading SK C/28 guns. These fired a 45.3kg (100lb) shell with separate charges. Their maximum rate of fire was eight rounds per minute and the maximum range was 23,000m (12.4 NM).

By the 1930s, all cruisers carried secondary batteries which could be used for anti-aircraft as well as anti-shipping duties. Typically, on British cruisers these were 4in. guns, such as the one in this photo. On German ships the similarly sized 105mm gun was used. These sailors are pictured loading ready ammunition into the gun's shot locker. (AC)

SHELLS

A heavy cruiser's main weapons were its guns. This plate shows the types of rounds carried by German and British heavy cruisers.

1. A cutaway of a British semi-armour-piercing 8in. shell for the British Mark VIII 8in. gun. This round used by County-class and York-class cruisers was similar to all German heavy gun projectiles. The ballistic cap on the front of the shell assured minimum wind resistance. Inside the cap was a bag filled with coloured dye, to mark the fall of the shot. The bag was detonated by the nose fuse when the shell struck the water. Behind the bag was a penetrator cap to slice through armour plate. The round contained a steel shell casing filled with explosive. It was detonated by the base fuse after the shell penetrated.

2. A British 4in. AA shell.
3. A British SAP 8in. shell.
4. A German armour-piercing 280mm shell.
5. A German HE 203mm shell.
6. A German armour-piercing 150mm shell.
7. A German 100mm AA shell.

The Germans colour-coded their shells, painting armour-piercing shells blue, high-explosive shells yellow, inert shells red and star-shells green. The small rounds (4in. and 100mm) were unitary, with projectile and propellant in one piece to permit rapid fire. The larger guns (150mm–280mm in diameter) used separate projectiles and propellant, with the propellant in separate bags or cartridges, loaded in the gun after the projectile was rammed home.

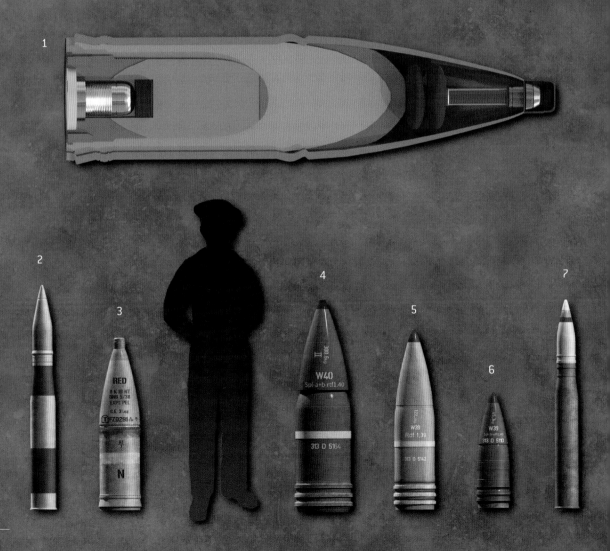

TORPEDO MOUNTS

While guns had the longer reach, a heavy cruiser's torpedoes were its deadliest weapon. A single torpedo had the potential to sink a heavy cruiser. Two or three torpedo hits would doom a heavy cruiser. Both German and British heavy cruisers carried torpedoes between 1939 and 1943.

The torpedoes were launched from deck-mounted torpedo tubes that could be aimed. British County-class cruisers and German *Panzerschiffe* carried eight torpedoes on two quadruple mounts. British York-class cruisers and German Admiral Hipper-class heavy cruisers carried triple mounts: two for the Yorks, for a total of six tubes, and four on the Hippers for a total of twelve. A cruiser could only fire half the torpedoes it carried from each broadside.

Torpedoes were slow and short-ranged. German cruiser torpedoes had a maximum range of 8,750yd (8,000m) at their 40kn setting. British cruiser torpedoes could reach 5,700yd (5,200m) at 35kn. They carried a 740–800lb warhead.

Heavy cruisers fired torpedoes at both the Battle of the River Plate and the Christmas Day Battle. No hits were scored on either occasion. *Blücher* was sunk by torpedoes. HMS *Dorsetshire* fired torpedoes credited with sinking the *Bismarck* at the end of *Bismarck*'s final battle. They were used so infrequently the Royal Navy began removing them from British cruisers to allow bigger anti-aircraft batteries.

These two illustrations show County-class cruiser HMS *Norfolk* and KMS *Prinz Eugen*. The two faced each other at the Denmark Strait, but did not fire their torpedoes in that battle.

The starboard torpedo mount on County-class cruiser HMS *Norfolk*.

The aft port torpedo mount on KMS *Prinz Eugen*.

FLOATPLANES

British and German heavy cruisers were equipped with floatplanes. Single-engine aircraft equipped with pontoons or built-in amphibian bodies, they were launched from cruisers' catapults and recovered after they landed on the water near the ship. British cruisers carried Fairey Seafox or Supermarine Walrus aircraft. German cruisers carried the monoplane Arado 196.

Floatplanes permitted cruisers operating independently in remote areas an aerial reconnaissance capability. They could also be used for gunnery spotting, allowing cruisers to fire over smokescreens or beyond the horizon. They could even be used to attack other ships. A floatplane from the battleship HMS *Warspite* torpedoed and sank a U-boat during the 1940 Norwegian campaign.

However, floatplanes had several drawbacks. The aircraft were fragile. Hangars and catapults for operating them took up space, and added weight to ships that were limited by treaty, leaving it unavailable for other uses. Superstructure-mounted catapults also caused stability problems. Additionally, the aircraft were run with volatile gasoline, creating a fire hazard in a surface action.

Occasionally useful, their drawbacks eventually led to the removal of aircraft from cruisers. Aircraft carriers became more available as the war progressed. Carrier aircraft were used for scouting, with space aboard cruisers used for additional anti-aircraft protection.

The Arado Ar 196 floatplane on *Admiral Graf Spee* wrecked by gunfire after the Battle of the River Plate. (AC)

All carried batteries of heavy anti-aircraft guns, the British cruisers and Hipper-class cruisers as secondary batteries. Dual-purpose guns, they were capable of engaging surface targets as well as aircraft, and could be useful against another heavy cruiser.

By World War II, British heavy cruisers mounted the Mark XVI or Mark XVII 4in. quick-firing guns on single or twin mounts. These entered service in 1936. They fired a 35.9lb shell, with a maximum rate of fire of 20 rounds per minute. Their maximum surface range was 21,300yd (10.5 NM), while maximum effective altitude as an anti-aircraft gun was 39,000ft (11,900m). While the *Deutschland* and *Admiral Scheer* were originally armed with an 88mm Flak battery, this was replaced in 1940 with the 105mm SK C/33 carried by *Admiral Graf Spee* and Hipper-class cruisers. A 65-calibre weapon, it fired a 15.1kg (33.3lb) round, and had a maximum rate of fire of 18 rounds per minute. Its maximum surface range was 17,600m (9.5 NM) and its maximum effective ceiling was 11,400m (37,400ft).

Heavy cruisers also carried lighter anti-aircraft guns. These included the British Vickers 40mm pompom and 0.5in. machine gun and German 37mm SK C/30 and 20mm/65 C/30 and 20mm/65 C/38 Flak guns. However, these had neither the range nor firepower to play an important role in a cruiser duel.

The final weapon carried by heavy cruisers of both sides was the torpedo. British heavy cruisers carried the 21in. Mark V natural air torpedo or the Mark VIIC oxygen-enriched torpedo. The Mark V entered service in 1918, and carried a 750lb TNT warhead. It had a 5,000yd range at 40kn, and 13,500yd range at 25kn. The Mark VII had a 740lb warhead with a range of 5,700yd and a speed of 35kn. Some cruisers replaced their Mark VII torpedoes with the Mark IX. The Mark IX had a 750lb warhead with a range of 10,500yd at 36kn, or 13,500yd at 30kn.

German ships carried the 533mm (21in.) G7a T1 torpedo introduced in 1938. These had a 280kg (617lb) Hexanite warhead. Highly reliable torpedoes, with outstanding performance, they could travel 6,000m (6,560yd) at 44kn, 8,000m (8,750yd) at 40kn, and 14,000m (15,300yd) at 30kn.

ELECTRONICS

World War II was the first conflict in which battlefield electronics played a significant role. Radar and radar jamming became important in battle. Both British and German warships mounted radar during the war's cruiser duels, although only British cruisers used ship-based direction finding and radio homing. The Kriegsmarine led the 'Wizard War' (as Churchill termed it) in 1939. As 1942 ended, Britain had a decisive edge.

The Kriegsmarine was an early adopter of radar, installing them on their cruisers long before the Royal Navy did on its ones. This is a picture of the antenna for a FuMO 27 gunnery control radar aboard *Prinz Eugen*. Germany lagged behind in radar development during the war and was eventually surpassed by the Allies. (USNHHC)

Germany began the war with radars mounted on all capital ships. It developed the Seetakt radar in 1935. It used a 500MHz frequency, and could spot aircraft up to a 28km (15.1 NM) distance. It could also track surface targets up to 8km (4.3 NM) distant to an accuracy of 50m, sufficient for gun ranging. A later model increased that to 22km (12 NM).

The first production version was labelled FGM 39 (*Funkmessgerät*), but is more widely known by its late-war designation of FuMO (*Funkmess Ordnung*) 22. These used a 2x6m or 2x4m mattress antenna. A later version, FuMO 27, was used for gunnery control, and was generally installed on the aft gun directors of ships that had it. Germany also developed passive radar systems which used enemy radar for detection. They were codenamed for tropical islands: Timor, Palau, Bali and Sumatra. These were used later in the war, and were not installed until late 1941 or early 1942.

Deutschland, fitted with a Seetakt set in autumn 1937, may have been the first warship with radar. All three Deutschland-class cruisers had FuMO 22 radar installed in 1939, as did *Admiral Hipper*. The latter's sisters entered service carrying FuMO 22 radar, with *Prinz Eugen* having a FuMO 27 radar and Sumatra and Timor antennae as well. *Lützow* received a Timor antenna in January 1943. *Admiral Scheer* added a FuMO 27 radar on both gun directors and Timor and Sumatra antennae in 1941. *Admiral Hipper* carried a FuMO 27 radar and Timor antenna after a refit in late 1941–early 1942.

Britain entered the radar race later. It began experimenting with radar in 1937, testing Type 97 radar. It was primarily air-search radar, operating at 43MHz, with a range of 30–50 miles (50–80km). The first operational radars were installed on the light cruiser HMS *Sheffield* in September 1939. Improved radars followed: Type 279 and Type 281 in 1940. Type 279 had a range of 50 NM as an air-search system. Type 281 could detect aircraft up to 115 NM distant, and had surface targeting capability. Type 286 could also be used for air and surface search. It had a surface range of 20 NM. More relevant to cruiser duels was the Type 284 radar. A gunnery radar, with a 10-mile (16km) range, it became operational in June 1940 and was installed on British battleships and heavy cruisers. It could be used for both gunnery direction and tracking surface ships.

No British heavy cruiser began World War II with radar, but the Royal Navy placed a high priority on adding this capability. HMAS *Australia* had Type 286 radar in November 1940. HMS *Suffolk* had types 279, 284 and 285 radar by February 1941. HMS *Exeter* received Type 279 radar while under repair after the 1939 Battle of the River Plate. HMS *Berwick* had type 281 and 284 radar added in a May 1941 refit, HMS *Kent* during repairs in September 1941. HMS *Cumberland* was first fitted for radar in October 1941, HMS *London* in January 1942, HMS *Shropshire* in June 1942 and HMS *Sussex* by August 1942. HMS *Norfolk* received types 281, 273, 284 and 285 radar in July 1942. HMAS *Canberra* and HMSs *Cornwall*, *Dorsetshire* and *York* never received radar.

Despite the late start, the Royal Navy used radar more aggressively than Germany. British radars outperformed German radars in both air search and gunnery by 1940. The Kriegsmarine, more conservative about developing radar, became reluctant to use active radar, fearing passive tracking.

THE COMBATANTS

The combatants who fought cruiser duels during World War II came from similar but different traditions and heritages. Sailors in the centuries prior to the 20th century were an international group. Then it would not be unusual for a warship to contain crewmen from a dozen different nations other than the ship's nationality. By World War II Royal Navy and Kriegsmarine crews were largely made up of inhabitants of their respective nations. They were national navies, reflecting their respective nations' characteristics. Yet the traditions of the two nations were vastly different. Britain had a representative government with free-market traditions. Nazi Germany was an authoritarian dictatorship, with a command economy.

By the mid-third of the 20th century sailors had changed in other ways. During the age of sail, sailing was a complex activity requiring skilled mariners. By 1939 the skills required had changed, and were even more complex than 150 years earlier. Steam (and diesel) propulsion and steel construction imposed new disciplines on sailors. They had to master the complex machinery of the power plant driving the ship, and work in metal rather than wood. They also needed to be skilled with electricity, compressed air, and power tools.

Weapons changed, too. The smoothbore cannon of the Napoleonic era firing sold shot had given way to rifled breechloaders, firing explosive and armour-piercing shells. Although the gun barrels weighed tons and fired rounds too heavy for men to lift, they were precision implements, requiring exact design tolerances. They required complex machinery to load, aim and fire. The 20th-century gunner had to be a man of great technical knowledge.

One thing had not changed: the sea. The hazards of the sea remained, waiting to kill the careless or the unwary. Even a 10,000-ton warship could prove helpless before

The peacetime Royal Navy was an all-volunteer force. Even during wartime, the men who served in it volunteered for the Navy in preference to serving in the Army. Here, new recruits go through inspection early in their training. (AC)

the fury of a storm, an unexpected iceberg, or an uncharted reef. The sailors who operated the German and British heavy cruisers which duelled in World War II had to be several things. They had to be masters of the technology of ships and warfare. Officers and men had to be consummate seamen, and skilled warriors used to working as a team. Both sides had these men.

THE ROYAL NAVY TAR

The Royal Navy could trace its lineage back to the Tudor era. It possessed a legacy of victory which began with the Spanish Armada in the 16th century, continuing through the age of fighting sail in the 19th century, and culminating in triumph over the German High Seas Fleet in World War I. The Royal Navy did not win all its battles, but always won the ones that counted. It went on to own the oceans. It achieved this through a pugnacious willingness to fight. Over a century after Horatio Nelson's death, men of the Royal Navy were still guided by his instructions given before the Battle of Trafalgar: 'No captain can do very wrong if he places his ship alongside that of the enemy.' The Royal Navy – officer and sailor – went into battle expecting to win.

In World War II, the Royal Navy was made up of a mixture of long-serving professionals and hostilities-only personnel. When the war began, it consisted of 200,000 men (including Marines and reserves). By the time it ended, there were nearly 1 million men in the Royal Navy, a five-fold increase.

Pre-war personnel were all volunteers. Except during wartime, the Royal Navy never used conscription. Even during wars, the Royal Navy preferred volunteers. Despite myths about impressment, even during the Napoleonic era, over half the sailors in the Royal Navy volunteered for service. Britain had instituted conscription during World War I, and in May 1939 reinstituted limited conscription, before broadening it when war broke out that September. Thereafter, everyone who entered military service could be considered a conscript, even if they intended to volunteer.

BADGES OF THE ROYAL NAVY AND ROYAL MARINES

The badges are as follows : 1, Petty Officer ; 2, Leading Seaman ; 3, Gunner's Mate ; 4, Director Layer ; 5, Captain of Gun (1st Class); 6, Good Conduct (13 years' service and over; two stripes, 8 years' and under 13; one stripe, 3 years' and under 8); 7, Torpedo Gunner's Mate ; 8, Torpedo Coxswain ; 9, Leading Torpedo Man ; 10, Chief Petty Officer, Petty Officer, Leading Seaman, Seaman Torpedo Man ; 11, Chief Petty Officer, Petty Officer, Leading Seaman, and Seaman Gunner ; 12, Range Taker (1st Class); 13, Visual Signalman (1st Class) ; 14, Visual Signalman (3rd Class) ; 15, Signalman ; 16, Diver ; 17, Observer's Mate ; 18, Chief Photographer ; 19, Mechanician ; 20, Chief Petty Officer, Petty Officer Stoker ; 21, Leading Stoker, Stoker (1st Class) ; 22, Wireless Telegraphist (1st Class) ; 23, Wireless Telegraphist (3rd Class) ; 24, Surveying Recorder ; 25, Submarine Detector Instructor ; 26, Submarine Detector Operator ; 27, Physical and Recreational Training Instructor (1st Class) ; 28, Chief Armourer, Armourer ; 29, Chief Shipwright ; 30, Regulating Petty Officer ; 31, Writer ; 32, Supply Rating ; 33, Master-at-Arms ; 34, Sick Berth Attendant ; 35, Marksman (musketry) ; 36, Bugler.

By World War II, service in the Royal Navy was technical and often highly specialized. These badges represent the skills enlisted personnel could earn through training and experience. They often required specialized training, sometimes combined with years of experience. (AC)

However, conscripts could select the service they wished to join. The Royal Navy always got more volunteers than it needed, selecting those that were physically the best, and the best educationally qualified.

Before World War II, sailors were recruited in their late teens, going through training as boys, and entering service at age 18 for a 12-year hitch. If they performed satisfactorily, they could enlist for ten more years, and retire at age 40 with a pension. They trained at shore training establishments, like HMS *Ganges* (shore establishments were accorded the dignity of being labelled 'HMS' – His Majesty's Ship). Hard economic times during the 1930s ensured a steady flow of recruits. The system ended with World War II, due to increased manpower requirements. The last class of boy seamen was admitted in 1940. Thereafter, training focused on hostilities-only recruits brought in during the war.

Hostilities-only recruits were older: men between 18 and 41 through 1941 and up to 46 years old beginning in 1942. Initially, the intake was limited, due to a lack of training bases, but by 1942, 17 training camps were open. Some were peacetime summer camps, repurposed to training facilities. Wartime basic training at these camps initially took four months, but was eventually compressed to only seven weeks. There recruits learned basic seamanship and naval protocol, and went through physical conditioning. Thereafter, they were sent for advanced training based on specialty.

Over one-third became seamen, trained for deck operations. Another 20 per cent were trained as stokers, working in the engine rooms. These were the strongest men, as the work was viewed as requiring more physical stamina. The remainder became stewards, cooks, sick-berth attendants, telegraphists (radiomen) or writers. In theory, specialists were chosen based on intelligence, aptitude and previous experience. In practice, assignments were made based on the needs of the service. Any selected men were sent to advanced schools where they learned the skills of that trade. Seamen and stokers also went through advanced training. Seamen could train in gunnery, torpedoes, communications or radar/Asdic operation. Stokers (who no longer stoked coal) learned about engine-room machinery (boilers and engines) or trained as artificers (mechanics). In each case they were sent to a training school for up to four months, the length of time dependent upon the complexity of training.

Gunners were divided into quarter ratings, gun layers and control ratings. Torpedo training included mines and depth charges, and incorporated electrician training. Communications Branch trainees learned visual signalling (with flags and signal lamps) or wireless telegraphy. Similarly, men using radar and Asdic equipment went through training in both shore- and ship-based training establishments. Promising stokers could become artificers. Artificers learned mechanical, marine and electrical engineering, in specialized training that could last up to four years; they could become engineering petty officers. Seamen with ability and experience would be promoted into positions of authority aboard a ship as petty officers and chief petty officers.

Officers typically followed a different career path than enlisted ranks, although by World War II, petty officers were given commissions. Typically, though, officers entered the Royal Navy on an officer track. There were three categories of officers in the Royal Navy: Regular Navy, Royal Naval Reserve and Royal Naval Volunteer Reserve.

Regular officers typically attended the Royal Naval College, Dartmouth, also known as HMS *Britannia*. Until 1921 (when it closed), cadets originally joined the

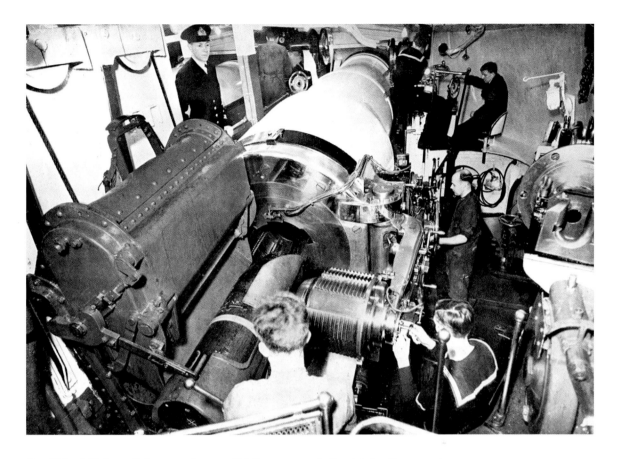

Royal Naval College, Osborne at the age of 13 for two years before joining Dartmouth. Cadets spent four years at Dartmouth, before starting sea training at 17, and service as midshipmen. Dartmouth provided the academic background expected of officers, and placement in the final exam influenced their careers. Unlike the US Naval Academy, Dartmouth cadets paid to attend during this period. Regular Royal Navy officers provided the senior leadership in the Royal Navy, and commanded most major warships.

These officers were supplemented by the Royal Naval Reserve. Created in 1859, it was made up of professional mariners serving as officers in Britain's merchant marine and fishing fleet. These men went through a shore-based training course to learn gunnery and naval protocol before returning to civilian careers. During wartime, these men were mobilized into the Navy, filling subordinate slots in large warships (such as cruisers) and commanding smaller warships.

The third category, the Royal Naval Volunteer Reserve (RNVR), was created in 1903. It offered commissions to civilians interested in the sea who were not professional mariners. Starting in 1938, it also included civilian pilots interested in flying for the Fleet Air Arm. After World War II started, the RNVR became the mechanism for civilians interested in serving as hostilities-only officers to join the Royal Navy. Pre-war members of the RNVR or the Royal Naval Volunteer (Supplementary) Reserve (a register of volunteers with maritime or aviation experience – typically yachtsmen or pilots) were mobilized into the Royal Navy when

Gunnery training in the Royal Navy was conducted aboard old warships, such as this class being given aboard HMS *Iron Duke*. While the ships and guns on which training was conducted may have been obsolete, the principles learned were relevant to naval artillery in contemporary use. (AC)

FREDERICK SECKER BELL

Frederick Secker Bell, who commanded HMS *Exeter* at the Battle of the River Plate, had a life that sounds like it was taken from a boys' adventure story, right down to his nickname 'Hookey' from his prominent nose.

He was born in London on 17 August 1897, the youngest son of Colonel Frank Burnman Bell and his wife Minnie. He was educated at Marfield Grange in Kent. By 1910, he was at the Royal Naval College and attended both Osborne (on the Isle of Wight) and Dartmouth. At the start of World War I he was a midshipman, and served aboard cruisers HMSs *Cumberland* and *Challenger* off the West African Coast during the Cameroon campaign.

In 1916, he received his commission, joining the battleship HMS *Canada* in time to serve aboard her as a junior officer during the Battle of Jutland. He then switched to submarine service, becoming the second-in-command of submarine HMS *D6*. In June 1918, *D6* was sent to patrol the Irish coast near Donegal, to hunt and sink *UB-73*. Instead, a submerged *UB-73* spotted a surfaced *D6*, torpedoed it and sank it. The only survivors were Bell and *D6*'s captain, who were taken aboard *UB-73* as prisoners. Bell spent the rest of the war in a POW camp in Germany.

Between the wars, Bell spent much of his time at sea, from 1923 to 1925 as 1st lieutenant of HMS *Scythe* off Ireland. After that he served on the China Station. In 1930, he was loaned to the Royal Australian Navy. He served aboard HMAS *Australia* (a County-class cruiser) and then as Director of Naval Intelligence at Melbourne. He was promoted to commander in 1931. He met his wife, Dulcie Carmel Cohen, in Australia, although they married in Portsmouth in 1935, after his return to Britain. Back in the Royal Navy, he attended the Naval War College. He became second-in-command of the battlecruiser HMS *Repulse* for three years in the late 1930s when *Repulse* was in the Mediterranean.

Promoted to captain in January 1939, he took command of HMS *Exeter* in August 1939. *Exeter* was assigned to the South American Division when World War II broke out, and spent the rest of 1939 tracking down German surface raiders in the South Atlantic, participating in the Battle of the River Plate on 13 December 1939.

Bell returned to Britain with the heavily damaged HMS *Exeter*, receiving a hero's welcome. He was knighted a Companion of the Bath (CB). As *Exeter* was undergoing lengthy repairs, Bell was reassigned. In 1941, he was Flag Captain to Flag Officer Malaya. Before Singapore fell, Bell escaped, 'borrowing' a boat from the Singapore Yacht Club and taking it to Sumatra. From there he was evacuated to Australia.

He commanded the battleship HMS *Anson* in 1946, becoming aide-de-camp to King George VI in 1947. He retired from the Royal Navy in 1948 due to ill health. After the war, in retirement, he served as technical advisor to the film *The Battle of the River Plate*, where he was played by John Gregson. He died on 23 November 1973, aged 76.

Captain Frederick Bell. (AC)

World War II began, going through a ten-day orientation course. Thereafter, wartime RNVR officer candidates went through a 12-week officer training course before earning commissions.

These three classes of officers used the same rank structure – the traditional one of sub-lieutenant, lieutenant, lieutenant-commander, commander and captain. They were differentiated by their sleeve insignia. Regular Navy officers had straight rank rings, RNR officers had braided rings and RNVR officers wavy rings (leading to their nickname of the 'Wavy Navy'). All were professional and capable officers, even if new RNVR officers lacked experience.

THE KRIEGSMARINE *SEEMANN*

While the Royal Navy had centuries of tradition to fall back upon, the Kriegsmarine was a much newer service. Its origins dated to the creation of the Kaiserliche Marine (Imperial German Navy), formed in 1871. By 1939, the Kaiserliche Marine changed its name twice: to Reichsmarine in 1919 and Kriegsmarine in 1935 – yet it was much the same organization. Most of the Kriegsmarine's senior officers in World War II started their service in the Kaiserliche Marine and were combat veterans of World War I.

Unlike the Royal Navy with a tradition of naval victories against desperate odds, the Kriegsmarine's leaders tended to celebrate glorious last stands. While it did achieve victories, notably at Coronel and in the Baltic, they proved transitory. Its most celebrated events were successful retreats or – as in the scuttling of the High Seas Fleet at Scapa Flow after World War I – actions to deny their enemies German resources.

When World War II began, the Kriegsmarine was an all-volunteer service. Compared to the Wehrmacht or Luftwaffe, its manpower demands were small, so it remained all-volunteer throughout the war. Recruits joined the Kriegsmarine when they were between 17 and 23 years of age. Those under 21 needed parental permission. Recruits had to be physically fit, in good health (including good teeth) and of at least average intelligence. They also had to demonstrate German nationality, and that they had completed secondary education. A criminal record barred enlistment. Applicants were drawn from all over Germany, both inland and coastal regions.

Those who served in the merchant marine or possessed appropriate technical skills (including having completed apprenticeships) in mechanics and electricity were preferred. Since the Kriegsmarine was small, it could be picky about those who wished to join. High German unemployment before the war, and preferring naval service to the army during the war, ensured a surplus of applicants.

Recruits joined for at least five years (the first of which was training), becoming *Matrosen* (sailors). Once in the Kriegsmarine, recruits were assigned to one of 12 specialties, which ranged from seaman to coastal artilleryman. Half were assigned as the former. Others specialized in skills needed in the engine rooms, to man the helm, operate the weapons or administer paperwork. A few became medical orderlies or musicians.

Kriegsmarine recruits went through the same basic training as Wehrmacht infantry, right down to wearing army *feldgrau* uniforms and practising infantry drill and

All Kriegsmarine sailors started their enlistment by going through basic infantryman training. They could double as infantrymen in a pinch, such as this landing party that helped occupy the British Channel Islands in World War II. (AC)

weapons training. After completing this training, they were passed to specialist training schools in Kiel, Mürwick or Swinemünde. From there they were posted to service assignments. Trained recruits were given the rank of *Matrose* (ordinary seaman). After a year's service, the *Matrose* could expect promotion to *Matrosengefreiter* (able seaman). Long-service men, those with at least five years' service as a *Matrosengefreiter*, could receive promotion to *Matrosenhauptgefreiter* (high able seaman). The rank carried no extra pay or responsibility, but offered extra respect and prestige.

Promotion to petty officer or *Maat* depended on the recommendation of an officer. Men accepting promotion lengthened their career obligation from four years to 12. During wartime or periods of rapid expansion, promising recruits could be offered an opportunity to become a *Maat* after basic training. Those accepting promotion to *Maat* after completing basic training went to their specialist training first. Every candidate for promotion to *Maat* went to the *Marineunteroffizierlehrabteilung* (petty officer school) at either Friedrichsort or (after 1938) in Wesermünde (in Bremerhaven). There they went through leadership and combat training given by army NCOs, again donning *feldgrau* uniforms, and simulated land combat.

After three years as a *Maat*, a sailor could receive promotion to *Obermate*. Senior enlisted personnel could become warrant officers (the equivalent of senior petty officers in the US and Royal navies). There were three tracks: one for shore-based personnel, one for deck personnel and one for navigation specialists. The titles differed for each track. They formed the backbone of a Kriegsmarine ship. The most senior warrant ranks were given to those considered good enough to retain after completing their 12-year service obligation.

The officers of the Kaiserliche Marine were drawn from Germany's patricians and upper-middle classes. Although Kaiserliche Marine veterans dominated the upper ranks of the Reichsmarine and Kriegsmarine, officers joining after 1919 came from more egalitarian backgrounds, passing through the recruitment process similar to those of the enlisted personnel. Along with demonstrating German background, officer candidates also had to provide information on their parents and grandparents, to ensure they too were properly German.

Officer training was rigorous, as it always had been. A Kriegsmarine officer was expected to be a competent seaman and navigator as well as a leader. They went through the same basic training as *Matrosen*, and then four months of practical training, depending on their career specialty. Officers followed one of four career paths: they could be a line officer (*Offizier zur See*), an engineering officer (*Ingenieur*), weapons specialist (*Waffen-offizier*) or a member of the administrative staff.

A Kriegsmarine signalman projects the desired image of the Kriegsmarine *Seemann* – an exemplary specimen of German youth, physically fit, intelligent and competent. (AC)

Upon completion of this training, they were promoted to cadet, serving nine months on a training ship. Eighteen months of advanced training followed for line and engineering candidates (two years for gunnery officers) followed by six months of fleet service. Only then were they promoted to *Leutnant* (lieutenant – equivalent to a Royal Navy or US Navy ensign). From then on, the promotion sequence was *Oberleutnant* (lieutenant, junior grade), *Kapitänleutnant* (lieutenant), *Korvettenkapitän* (lieutenant-commander), *Fregattenkapitän* (commander) and *Kapitän* (captain). A *Kapitän* commanded heavy cruisers or larger warships.

While the Wehrmacht was reactionary and the Luftwaffe actively National Socialist, the Kriegsmarine was the least politically active branch of the German armed forces. It remaining largely apolitical through the period in which it was commanded by Grossadmiral Erich Raeder, from its creation in 1935 until Raeder stepped down in January 1943. This continued the tradition set by the Kaiserliche Marine. For many years, Kriegsmarine officers were prohibited from being members of a political party. This changed under Karl Dönitz, when he replaced Raeder. Officer candidates who belonged to the Nazi Party had to resign membership before accepting a commission.

A sailor's job included hard physical effort, especially in the engine room or handling ammunition. An engine room seaman pulls a 110kg burner from a steam-plant boiler for inspection and servicing. He is wearing a leather engine-room suit. (AC)

German naval officers and sailors were patriotic and viewed themselves as fierce defenders of the Fatherland, regardless of the party in power. The Kriegsmarine, especially those in its heavy surface units, viewed honourable behaviour seriously. While determined to defeat the Royal Navy, Kriegsmarine personnel maintained great respect for their British opponents. They fought hard, but viewed their maritime foes as fellow mariners and adversaries, rather than enemies.

The Kriegsmarine entered World War II with experienced, well-trained crews and a professional, technically competent officer corps. Its members believed they belonged to an elite branch of Germany's armed forces. Rations and living conditions were considered better than in the Wehrmacht, and you generally went into battle having slept in your bed and with a stomach full of warm food. Despite Germany's naval build-up between 1935 and 1939, the Kriegsmarine was still relatively small when the war started, and its contingent of large ships increased within planned limits.

WILHELM MEISEL

Wilhelm Meisel was the Kriegsmarine's most successful World War II cruiser commander. He was born on 4 November 1891 in Zwickau in Saxony, and joined the Imperial German Navy as a midshipman in 1913. During World War I, he served aboard several ships, including SMS *Kaiserin Augusta*, a gunnery training ship, the battlecruiser SMS *Moltke* and light cruiser *Stralsund*. Meisel also served as an officer aboard SMS *Möwe*, a disguised surface raider.

Meisel then served as a staff officer in a torpedo-boat unit. Sent to Scapa Flow after the Armistice, Meisel participated in the 21 June 1919 scuttling of the High Seas Fleet. He was subsequently interned as a POW, being repatriated to Germany in 1921. Meisel was retained in the post-war Reichsmarine due to his outstanding war record. His service in the Reichsmarine appears concentrated in torpedo boats and destroyers. He commanded a torpedo boat flotilla in the 1920s, then served in various staff positions.

In August 1939, Meisel commanded the First Destroyer Flotilla (1.Zerstörerflottille). He directed its operations during the invasion of Poland. Afterwards, he served as the acting leader of torpedo boats (the Kriegsmarine's destroyers and torpedo boats). On 9 September 1940, Meisel assumed command of KMS *Admiral Hipper*, his first cruiser command. On 29 September 1940, Meisel and *Admiral Hipper* sailed from Kiel on its first attempt at a raiding cruise. Mechanical issues forced the ship to abort the mission and return for repairs. Meisel tried again, departing Germany in late November, and breaking into the Atlantic through the Denmark Strait on 7 December 1940.

Meisel failed to find *Admiral Hipper*'s intended targets, Convoys HX 93 and SC 15. Instead, on Christmas Eve, he intercepted troop convoy WS 5A. He attacked the next morning, only to discover its escort included three cruisers, including heavy cruiser HMS *Berwick*. After a brief battle, Meisel broke off. Experiencing engine problems, his ship then returned to France, sinking a freighter on the way.

Admiral Hipper's second cruise in February 1940 was more successful. Meisel caught and sank a straggler from Convoy HG 53. He then encountered Convoy SLS 64. He sank seven of the convoy's 18 ships, and damaged three others. Again experiencing engine problems, Meisel ended

the cruise, docking at Brest. After repairs at Brest, Meisel took *Admiral Hipper* back to Germany, departing Brest on 15 March, and arriving at Kiel on the 28th.

Meisel remained in command of *Admiral Hipper* through to October 1942, overseeing a lengthy refit. Sent to Norway in March 1942, Meisel participated in Operation *Rösselsprung* (the attempt to trap Arctic convoy PQ 17) and a subsequent abortive operation against PQ 18. Promoted to *Admiral*, he left *Admiral Hipper*, serving as Chief of Staff of Naval Group West in 1943 before being promoted to Chief of Staff of the Seekriegsleitung (Maritime Warfare Command) in February 1943, and succeeding Karl Dönitz as the Commander of the Seekriegsleitung on 1 May 1944, a position he held until the war's end.

Discharged from the Kriegsmarine when it disbanded in July 1945, he went into retirement. He died, age 82, in Mülheim, West Germany on 7 September 1974.

Kapitän Wilhelm Meisel. (Wikipedia)

COMBAT

German and British heavy cruisers fired at each other on only three occasions: the Battle of the River Plate in December 1939, the 1940 Christmas Day Battle between *Admiral Hipper* and HMS *Berwick* and in the Denmark Strait in May 1941. They had nearly encountered each other on a further occasion: in July 1942, when the Kriegsmarine launched Operation *Rösselsprung*, an attempt to trap convoy PQ 17. British and German cruisers sparred at the Battle of the Barents Sea in December 1942; on that occasion, a German heavy cruiser fought British light cruisers, with no heavy cruisers participating.

There were several reasons for this scarcity of actions. One was the small number of German ships rated as heavy cruisers. Only three *Panzerschiffe* and one heavy cruiser were in commission when the war began. One *Panzerschiff* was lost in 1939. The second heavy cruiser commissioned was lost in May 1940, shortly after it entered service. Only one other heavy cruiser was commissioned. That left Germany with no more than four ships rated as heavy cruisers (*Panzerschiffe* were re-rated as heavy cruisers in February 1940) available through most of the war. Refit and repair reduced the number operationally available at any time to two, sometimes only one.

Heavy cruisers were not intended to fight each other. The British heavy cruisers were created to hunt down lone surface raiders acting against British commerce on the high seas. Their designers anticipated most of these would be auxiliary cruisers, warships converted from merchant vessels, armed with guns up to 6in. in size. British heavy cruisers intercepted and sank two German auxiliary raiders, both in 1941. HMS *Cornwall* caught and sank the auxiliary cruiser *Pinguin* in the Indian Ocean on 8 May 1941. HMS *Cornwall* was 500 NM from *Pinguin* when the raider attacked a British merchant ship. It located *Pinguin* using the Walrus seaplanes HMS *Cornwall* carried. Similarly, on 22 November 1941, HMS *Devonshire* used signal intelligence to locate

A Royal Navy County-class cruiser steaming in home waters sometime in 1940. These ships were constantly at sea during World War II, protecting Britain's sea lanes. (AC)

the German raider *Atlantis*. *Devonshire* caught it north of Ascension Island in the South Atlantic, and sank the ship after a brief gun battle. Two weeks later, another County-class cruiser which had been searching for *Atlantis*, HMS *Dorsetshire*, found and sank *Python*, a German auxiliary which had served as a supply ship for *Atlantis*.

German raiders were not interested in fighting British warships. They were hunting lone merchantmen in waters without convoys, or seeking lightly guarded convoys without cruiser or battleship protection. Battle risked damage, which would cut raiding cruises short, or lead to the loss of the raider. Yet the enemy always gets a vote. The British were willing to fight heavy cruisers raiding the Atlantic and Indian oceans with their own heavy cruisers. They used their heavy cruisers to defend escorted convoys and to hunt down raiders. Given the huge sizes of the world's oceans, they only succeeded twice: at River Plate and on Christmas Day 1940. The action in the Denmark Strait was constrained by the presence of battleships; the two Arctic actions by a German reluctance to engage.

THE RIVER PLATE

The Battle of the River Plate was the first action between German and British heavy cruisers, and the first major surface action of World War II. It remains one of the best-known naval actions of that war.

Admiral Graf Spee during pre-war naval manoeuvres. Another Deutschland-class ship is behind it. Sent on a raiding cruise prior to the start of World War II, *Admiral Graf Spee* was tracked down by British cruisers and defeated in the South Atlantic Ocean. (AC)

In late August 1939, anticipating the war beginning in early September, Grossadmiral Raeder sent two of the Kreigsmarine's three *Panzerschiffe* into the Atlantic, along with supporting supply ships. They were to commence operations against Allied shipping when notified. *Deutschland* was assigned the North Atlantic, while *Admiral Graf Spee* was sent to the South Atlantic and Indian oceans. Permission to attack was sent at the end of September. *Admiral Graf Spee* opened the campaign on 30 September, sinking the British cargo/passenger liner SS *Clement*. On 5 October, *Deutschland* sank the British transport SS *Stonegate*.

Britain and France immediately dispatched groups of warships to hunt down the two raiders. These included Force F (HMSs *Berwick* and *York*) in North American and West Indies waters, Force G (HMSs *Exeter* and *Cumberland*, later reinforced by light cruisers HMSs *Ajax* and *Achilles*) in the South Atlantic, Force H (HMSs *Sussex* and *Shropshire*) to cover the Cape of Good Hope and Force I (HMSs *Cornwall* and *Dorsetshire*, accompanied by aircraft carrier HMS *Eagle*) to patrol the Indian Ocean from Ceylon. Additional forces included Force K (British carrier HMS *Ark Royal* and battlecruiser HMS *Renown*), and three French groups: Force L out of Brest with the battlecruiser *Dunkerque*, carrier *Béarn* and three light cruisers; Force M (heavy cruisers *Foch* and *Dupleix*) out of Dakar; and Force N (battlecruiser *Strasbourg* with British aircraft carrier HMS *Hermes*) in the West Indies.

Deutschland eluded detection, returning safely to Germany on 17 November, having sunk one additional merchant ship and capturing another for a total of three ships. Meanwhile, hunted by three British forces (G, H and K) and French forces M and N, *Admiral Graf Spee* eluded its pursuers for over two months. It was detected only when it sank another merchant ship, its victim having radioed a contact report with a position. Several times it used its aircraft to avoid pursuers. The British managed to capture three of *Admiral Graf Spee*'s supply ships, but missed an opportunity to take supply ship *Altmark* after encountering it.

In early December, Commodore Henry Harwood, commanding Force G, decided to catch *Admiral Graf Spee* through interception rather than pursuit. Realizing the German ship had not yet raided the prize-rich seas near the approaches to the River Plate, on 9 December he ordered his cruisers to concentrate 150 NM east of the river estuary. Harwood arrived at the rendezvous on 12 December, with cruisers *Exeter*, *Ajax* and *Achilles* (HMS *Cumberland* was at Port Stanley in the Falklands, refuelling). HMS *Exeter* had six 8in. main guns, while HMSs *Ajax* and

Achilles carried a main battery of eight 6in. guns, each firing a 112lb shell, half the weight of *Exeter*'s 8in. rounds.

Harwood's timing was perfect. The next morning, at 0608hrs, HMS *Ajax* reported smoke to the north-west. HMS *Exeter* was sent to investigate. At 0616hrs, it signalled, 'I think it is a pocket battleship.' It was *Admiral Graf Spee*. Conditions were perfect for a daytime gunnery battle. There was no haze and visibility exceeded 15 NM. The battle began at 0618hrs, when *Admiral Graf Spee* fired its main guns. The British cruisers split up, *Exeter* turning to port, while *Ajax* and *Achilles* continued ahead. Two minutes later, at a range of 19,400yd, HMS *Exeter* opened fire with its forward guns. Shortly thereafter, *Ajax* and *Achilles* joined in, opening fire at 19,200yd. HMS *Ajax* launched a Fairey Seafox seaplane for artillery spotting.

Admiral Graf Spee concentrated its 150mm secondary battery on the light cruisers, but split the main gun fire between the two groups. Failing to score hits with its main guns, it soon concentrated on HMS *Exeter*. It scored two quick hits at 0623hrs and 0624hrs. The second one knocked out *Exeter*'s superfiring 'B' turret. Two more hits landed forward at 0826hrs, blasting a 10ft x 10ft hole in the forecastle deck.

HMS *Exeter* fired its starboard torpedo tubes at *Admiral Graf Spee*, which turned to avoid them. At 0640hrs, another 280mm round struck the port gun of *Exeter*'s lead turret, knocking it out. HMS *Exeter* turned to starboard and fired its three port torpedoes. It was hit by a seventh shell, which struck forward of its lead starboard 4in. gun and detonated its ready ammunition. *Exeter*'s aft turret was forced to local gunnery control.

To distract *Admiral Graf Spee*, HMSs *Ajax* and *Achilles* closed range to 13,200yd, and concentrated fire on the *Panzerschiff*. It worked. *Admiral Graf Spee* began making smoke. The German ship, which had radar, could range through the smoke, and *Ajax* and *Achilles* were soon receiving 290mm fire. Both had several near misses, one of which knocked out HMS *Achilles*' radio. *Admiral Graf Spee* turned directly towards HMS *Exeter* at 0617hrs, prompting *Ajax* and *Achilles* to close even further, and blanket the *Panzerschiff* with accurate fire. *Admiral Graf Spee* turned to the north-west, away from HMS *Exeter*, and resumed firing on *Ajax*, which was hit at 0725hrs by a shell that knocked out its two aft turrets. By then, the light cruisers were only 7,000yd from *Admiral Graf Spee*. HMS *Ajax* fired its four port torpedoes at the German cruiser, which turned to avoid them.

At 0730hrs, HMS *Exeter* lost power to its aft turret, leaving it with no working main guns. At 0740hrs, Harwood broke off the action, after an erroneous report that HMS *Ajax* had only 20 per cent of its 6in. shells remaining. *Admiral Graf Spee* had done enough fighting for one day, and her captain Hans Langsdorff allowed the action to end. It had been struck by 20 large shells, including two 8in. rounds. Kapitän Langsdorff decided

Commodore Henry Harwood commanded a four-cruiser Royal Navy squadron in the South Atlantic. With three of these cruisers, he fought *Admiral Graf Spee* near the approaches to the River Plate. (AC)

SUPPLY SHIPS

One problem facing German cruisers raiding in the Atlantic and Indian oceans was supply. Refuelling was necessary, even for the diesel-powered, long-range *Panzerschiffe*, to say nothing of the short-legged Admiral Hipper-class vessels with their perpetually thirsty steam plants. Food and ammunition became issues on multi-month cruises.

The Royal Navy had a worldwide network of bases in which they could replenish their warships. The Kriegsmarine did not. Neutrality laws limited the fuel and supplies combatants could receive. Warships arriving at neutral ports also had their presence made known to opponents. Raiding German warships needed to avoid that kind of attention.

Instead, Germany created a network of covert supply ships. Disguised as merchant vessels, even though they were manned by Kriegsmarine crews, they could obtain fuel and non-military supplies in neutral ports. At sea they disguised their identities as neutral vessels. These ships, pre-positioned prior to the war's opening or sailing from German-occupied French ports, could even carry ammunition.

They were successful during the war's early years, when there was a larger number of neutral nations and fewer British air patrols over oceanic waters existed. Eventually, it became too difficult to operate Atlantic supply ships, especially after the US entry into the war, offering one reason why Kriegsmarine cruiser raids ceased after 1941.

The tanker *Altmark* was the most famous Kriegsmarine supply ship. It is shown here in Jøssingfjord, shortly after HMS *Cossack* raided *Altmark* to liberate British merchant seamen captured by *Admiral Graf Spee* that were being held prisoner aboard *Altmark*. (AC)

to take the ship into Montevideo harbour, in neutral Uruguay. One 8in. hit had damaged the oil purification plant, without which, Langsdorff feared, the ship could not make it back to Germany. The ship's desalination plant and galley had also been destroyed.

Admiral Graf Spee was shadowed into port by HMSs *Ajax* and *Achilles*, while HMS *Exeter* departed for the Falklands for repairs. HMS *Cumberland* arrived the next day, with Force H due to arrive on 19 December, and Force K soon after that. It did not matter. On 19 December 1939, rather than renew the fight, Kapitän Langsdorff scuttled *Admiral Graf Spee* in the River Plate estuary.

THE CHRISTMAS DAY BATTLE

The 25 December 1940 battle fought between the Kriegsmarine heavy cruiser *Admiral Hipper* and the defenders of convoy WS 5A was the closest thing to a precise duel between a German and a British heavy cruiser during World War II. Most of the fighting involved *Admiral Hipper* and the County-class heavy cruiser HMS *Berwick*. While light cruisers HMSs *Dunedin* and *Bonaventure* were present, they played little part in the battle. Due to rain and mist, *Admiral Hipper* was unaware HMS *Bonaventure*

was present and mistook HMS *Dunedin* for a destroyer. Its actions were motivated by *Berwick*'s presence.

On 25 November 1940, *Admiral Hipper* departed Kiel on a raiding cruise. Its objective was to intercept British convoys in the North Atlantic. Three sets of convoys were sought: eastbound HX and SC convoys to Britain originating in North America, and West African SL convoys sailing from Sierra Leone to Liverpool. HX convoys were 'fast' convoys for ships traveling at 9–13kn. The SC ones were 'slow' convoys for ships capable of only 8kn or less. According to German intelligence, the HX convoys sailed every four days and the SC convoys every 10 days.

Admiral Hipper's cruise got off to a frustrating start. A fleet oiler assigned to support the ship through the Denmark Strait (between Greenland and Iceland) had engine trouble and was forced to return to port. Hipper was forced to rely on two commandeered civilian tankers for refuelling, both of which sailed from French ports. Unable to refuel after leaving Norway until after it crossed the Denmark Strait, *Admiral Hipper* would be low on fuel until it rendezvoused with one of the French-based tankers.

Admiral Hipper was fortunate enough to slip through the Denmark Strait on 7 December 1940 without encountering British warships. By 10 December, *Admiral Hipper* was on the path crossed by HX convoys, and searching for the reported HX 93. That day, engine trouble forced Wilhelm Meisel, *Admiral Hipper*'s captain, to shut down the starboard shaft. The damage required a dockyard to repair. *Admiral Hipper* would finish the cruise on the remaining two shafts. This gave the ship a top speed of 25kn, enough to overtake a convoy, but below that of British cruisers.

Admiral Hipper was then so low on fuel it had barely enough to make it to Brest. Steaming to a rendezvous, it refuelled from the tanker *Breme* on 12 December, without finding HX 93. *Admiral Hipper* spent the next week vainly searching for convoys HX 94, HX 95 and SC 15. The weather was uncooperative, being too poor to permit *Admiral Hipper* to operate its aircraft. Its search radius was limited to the horizon, even with its surface search radar.

Finally, Kapitän Meisel decided to seek out the SL convoys, running from Freetown in Sierra Leone to Britain. Those routes were further south, where winter North Atlantic weather was better, and further east, bringing *Admiral Hipper* closer to French bases. Refuelling on 20 December, and sending *Breme* to a new, more southerly rendezvous, Kapitän Meisel moved east and south, hunting SL convoys, on 21 December.

Air searches between 21 and 23 December found nothing, with one Arado Ar 196 lost. *Admiral Hipper* refuelled again on the 23rd. The next day, bad weather resumed,

Admiral Hipper was the first heavy cruiser commissioned by the Kriegsmarine. It conducted two raiding cruises in the North Atlantic. During the first, it briefly battled with the British heavy cruiser HMS *Berwick*. (AC)

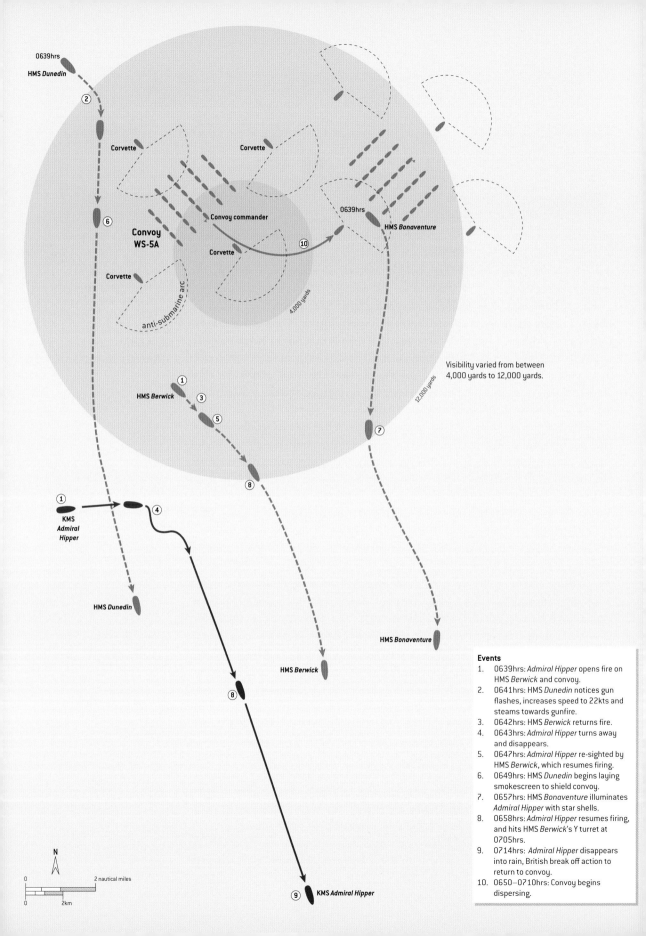

0639hrs
HMS *Dunedin*
②

Corvette   Corvette

Corvette

Convoy commander   ⑩   0639hrs

HMS *Bonaventure*

Corvette

Convoy
WS-5A   ⑥

Corvette

anti-submarine arc

4,000 yards

Visibility varied from between
4,000 yards to 12,000 yards.

①
HMS *Berwick*   ③
⑤

12,000 yards

⑦

⑧

①
KMS
*Admiral
Hipper*   ④

⑧

HMS *Dunedin*

HMS *Bonaventure*

HMS *Berwick*

N

0   2 nautical miles

0   2km

⑨ KMS *Admiral Hipper*

Events
1. 0639hrs: *Admiral Hipper* opens fire on
    HMS *Berwick* and convoy.
2. 0641hrs: HMS *Dunedin* notices gun
    flashes, increases speed to 22kts and
    steams towards gunfire.
3. 0642hrs: HMS *Berwick* returns fire.
4. 0643hrs: *Admiral Hipper* turns away
    and disappears.
5. 0647hrs: *Admiral Hipper* re-sighted by
    HMS *Berwick*, which resumes firing.
6. 0649hrs: HMS *Dunedin* begins laying
    smokescreen to shield convoy.
7. 0657hrs: HMS *Bonaventure* illuminates
    Admiral Hipper with star shells.
8. 0658hrs: *Admiral Hipper* resumes firing,
    and hits HMS *Berwick*'s Y turret at
    0705hrs.
9. 0714hrs: *Admiral Hipper* disappears
    into rain, British break off action to
    return to convoy.
10. 0650–0710hrs: Convoy begins
    dispersing.

but *Admiral Hipper*'s luck was in. Late in the afternoon of Christmas Eve, its radar picked up a surface contact, potentially a convoy. Closer examination proved it to be so. Since it was southbound, and the encounter was near the Azores, Kapitän Meisel assumed it was a lightly defended, outward-bound (OB) convoy from Britain to Africa. With nightfall approaching and wishing to be able to pursue the ships of the convoy in daylight, Meisel chose to shadow it throughout the night and attack at first light.

It was not an OB convoy. Rather, it was a WS convoy. These were fast troop convoys, used to express troops and military equipment to the Far East and Egypt. The code reputedly stood for 'Winston Special', as they were originally organized at Prime Minister Winston Churchill's desire to move troops quickly to remote locations requiring reinforcement. They were also heavily guarded. This particular convoy, WS 5A cruiser HMS *Berwick*, the World War I-era D-class light cruiser HMS *Dunedin* and the new anti-aircraft cruiser HMS *Bonaventure*. Also accompanying the convoy were aircraft carriers HMSs *Furious* and *Argus* ferrying crated aircraft for shipment to Egypt through West Africa. They carried only five flyable aircraft between them: three Skua dive-bombers aboard *Furious* and two Swordfish torpedo-bombers on *Argus*.

The only real match for *Admiral Hipper* was HMS *Berwick*. The elderly *Dunedin* was armed with only six single-mount 6in. guns and 12 torpedo tubes, and displaced 4,650 tons. The Dido-class HMS *Bonaventure* had a main battery of eight 5.25in. dual-purpose guns in twin mounts, with three turrets forward, and displaced 5,500 tons.

HMS *Berwick*, a Kent-class heavy cruiser, was escorting convoy WS 5A when the convoy was attacked by Kriegsmarine heavy cruiser *Admiral Hipper*. Although only two-thirds the displacement of the larger German cruiser, HMS *Berwick* attacked *Admiral Hipper* and successfully defended the convoy. (USNHHC)

OPPOSITE

The Christmas Day Battle, 25 December 1940.

Only HMS *Dunedin* had radar, a Type 286 set installed during a refit which ended a few days before it joined the convoy as an escort. HMS *Berwick* was fitted with radar during repairs after the battle, and HMS *Bonaventure*, despite being designed as an anti-aircraft ship, was sunk in March 1941 without ever receiving radar.

Admiral Hipper was ignorant of the escort as it tracked its quarry using radar. There was nothing to differentiate warships from merchantmen on the radar return. Since *Admiral Hipper* had not yet been detected, Kapitän Meisel decided to launch a torpedo attack on the convoy during the night, hoping that any hits would be mistaken for a U-boat attack. At 0153hrs, three torpedoes were launched from 5,000yd, based on radar ranging. All missed, and *Admiral Hipper* withdrew out of range of the convoy.

Christmas Day dawned with miserable weather. Weather conditions were poor, with heavy rain, Force 6 winds and rough seas. Visibility was 2 NM. *Admiral Hipper* closed in to visual range. Only then did Kapitän Meisel spot the distinctive three-funnel silhouette of a County-class cruiser. It was HMS *Berwick*, cleared for action at dawn stations, but unaware of the enemy's presence. *Admiral Hipper* fired three torpedoes at the cruiser, and broke away, until it became clear they had missed.

Admiral Hipper then closed to 6,000yd, and at 0639hrs opened fire on HMS *Berwick* at a range of 6,000yd. It shifted the fire of its secondary guns to the convoy, hitting two: SSs *Empire Trooper* and *Arabistan*. Two men aboard *Empire Trooper* were killed. HMS *Berwick* returned fire three minutes later, firing two broadsides at *Admiral Hipper*. Both salvos missed.

Both HMSs *Dunedin* and *Bonaventure* saw the gun flashes and closed to attack. *Bonaventure* opened up with its 5.25in. battery, but without effect. *Dunedin* had only one boiler on line, to save fuel. It could only make 22kn until its other boilers were brought up, a process that took 20 minutes. It then spent time laying a smoke screen to hide the convoy from the German raider. *Admiral Hipper* mistook both cruisers for destroyers and shifted its 105mm secondary battery to engage the two targets. It then turned away to avoid any torpedoes the 'destroyers' might fire, disappearing into the rain.

A running gunfight ensued, as *Admiral Hipper* attempted to break off the action. At 0647hrs, HMS *Berwick* spotted *Admiral Hipper* at 7,000yd and resumed fire, which *Admiral Hipper* returned. The latter began making smoke, which actually gave HMS *Berwick* an aiming point in the low light conditions. While *Admiral Hipper* could use its radar for ranging, HMS *Berwick* was firing optically, in extremely poor visibility.

The results were predictable. Not one of the 44 salvos fired by HMS *Berwick* scored a hit on *Admiral Hipper*. The German cruiser scored four hits on HMS *Berwick*, including one that knocked out its 'X' turret. Fortunately for HMS *Berwick*, only one exploded, on the uptake to the middle funnel.

By 0716hrs, HMS *Dunedin* was capable of making full speed. It closed at 28kn, intent on attacking *Admiral Hipper* with torpedoes. By then, *Admiral Hipper* was actively disengaging, retreating at its best speed. Rough seas forced HMS *Dunedin* to drop to 20kn, allowing *Admiral Hipper* to outpace it. In a similar fashion,

HMS *Dunedin* was part of the escort for WS 5A. *Admiral Hipper* mistook the elderly light cruiser for a destroyer. *Dunedin*'s presence contributed to *Admiral Hipper*'s decision to break off the action, as the latter's captain, Wilhelm Meisel, wished to avoid a destroyer's torpedo attack. [USNHHC]

HMS *Bonaventure* broke off combat as visibility worsened – as did HMS *Berwick*, which returned to its primary responsibility, protecting convoy WS 5A.

The aftermath was anticlimactic. The merchant ships of WS 5A scattered once it was clear they were being attacked by a surface raider. Three of the four escorting corvettes in the convoy spent the next few days reorganizing the convoy. SS *Empire Trooper* was escorted to Ponta Delgada in the Azores by the fourth corvette, HMS *Cyclamen*. HMS *Bonaventure* escorted SS *Arabistan* to safety.

The carriers HMSs *Furious* and *Argus* began searching for *Admiral Hipper*, a task complicated by the fact that *Argus*, carrying two Swordfish, only had bombs aboard, while *Furious*, with the Skuas, was only carrying torpedoes. HMS *Furious* launched its Skuas unarmed in search of *Admiral Hipper*, while HMS *Argus* transferred its Swordfish to *Furious* to be armed with torpedoes. When the Admiralty learned of the search, they ordered the carriers to break it off. This was perhaps fortunate. Had the lightly armed and protected carriers blundered across *Admiral Hipper* during their search, the cruiser could have easily sunk both.

And as for the *Admiral Hipper*? Kapitän Meisel decided he had done enough. On 22 December, the cruiser's propulsion began acting up again, with the bearings on the centre shaft running hot. If this had to be shut down, it would leave *Admiral Hipper* with one propeller and a top speed of 22kn. Again low on fuel, Kapitän Meisel pointed *Admiral Hipper*'s bow to Brest and the end of the mission. Along the way it came across the 6,000-ton merchant vessel *Jumna*, sailing independently after having left convoy OB 260. The heavy cruiser sank *Jumna*, giving it the only kill of the cruise before it made port at Brest on 27 December 1940.

THE DENMARK STRAIT

One other battle between German and British heavy cruisers was fought in 1941. It involved the British cruisers HMSs *Suffolk* and *Norfolk* and the German cruiser *Prinz Eugen* accompanying the battleship *Bismarck* on its ill-fated Atlantic sortie. Although the battle was a minor one, it was a significant milestone in cruiser warfare during the Battle of the Atlantic.

On 22 May 1941, having learned the *Bismarck* and *Prinz Eugen* were attempting to break into the Atlantic, the Royal Navy disposed its forces to intercept them as they crossed the Greenland–Iceland–Great Britain gap. The most likely passage was through the Denmark Strait, the path used by *Admiral Hipper* to enter and exit the Atlantic during its raiding cruises, although passage through other routes was possible and had to be covered.

The Dorsetshire-class HMS *Norfolk*, the newest of the County-class ships, was in the Denmark Strait. It was soon joined by the Kent-class HMS *Suffolk* on 22 May. HMS *Suffolk* was equipped with surface-search radar and had been using it for three months. The two ships were backed up by battleship HMS *Prince of Wales* and battlecruiser HMS *Hood* in Hvalfjord, Iceland.

In late May 1941, pack ice and minefields reduced the passage the German ships could take to a 35 NM channel. The two British cruisers spotted the German ships

late in the afternoon of 23 May, and began shadowing them, HMS *Suffolk* using its Type 284 radar and transmitting position reports. After being shadowed for 70 minutes, the Germans fired on their trackers, *Bismarck* on HMS *Suffolk*, *Prinz Eugen* on HMS *Norfolk*. The range was 5–6 NM.

The cruisers broke off. They continued stalking the Germans for the next nine hours, mostly using HMS *Suffolk*'s radar; occasionally through visual sightings by both cruisers. They stayed 15 NM behind the Germans, who were travelling at 28kn.

At 0552hrs on 24 May, HMSs *Hood* and *Prince of Wales*, which had entered the Denmark Strait searching for *Bismarck*, found the Germans. A 20-minute battle followed, in which *Hood* exploded and sank, while *Prince of Wales* was damaged and broke off.

The commander of the cruiser squadron, Rear Admiral Frederic Wake-Walker, took command of the surviving ships, and continued shadowing *Bismarck* and *Prinz Eugen*, waiting for the arrival of the British Home Fleet before attacking *Bismarck* again.

While tracking the Germans, *Prinz Eugen* appeared to fall back to attack HMS *Suffolk*. Radar reported *Prinz Eugen* 19,000yd from HMS *Suffolk*, while visual observation reported the German heavy cruiser at 24,000yd. At 0619hrs on 24 May, when radar reported *Prinz Eugen* at 12,400yd, HMS *Suffolk* opened fire, with six broadsides. It was then realized that the radar was tracking a reconnoitring aircraft, and fire ceased. Tracking continued.

Twelve hours later, at 1803hrs, *Bismarck* decided to trap HMS *Suffolk*. Disappearing into mist, it made a radical course change. At 1830hrs, it fired on *Suffolk* at 20,000yd. The rounds fell short. Ten minutes later, *Bismarck* resumed firing at the British heavy cruiser, which evaded and returned fire. *Bismarck*'s closest salvo landed 100yd from HMS *Suffolk*. The heavy cruiser straddled *Bismarck* with the third of nine broadsides it fired at the German battleship.

HMS *Prince of Wales* and *Prinz Eugen* joined the fight. *Prince of Wales* fired at *Bismarck*, which shifted target to the British battleship. *Prinz Eugen* opened fire, sending HMS *Suffolk* three broadsides. *Suffolk* returned fire – the last time German and British heavy cruisers would exchange fire. The Germans broke off at 1900hrs.

All of the firing was at long range and apparently radar-directed. The radarless HMS *Norfolk* stayed out of the fight. No damage was done to the enemy by either side, although the blast from HMS *Suffolk*'s main gun managed to shatter the heavy cruiser's bridge windows when firing on an extreme aft angle fleeing the *Bismarck*.

The cruisers' role in the battle ended six hours later. At 2330hrs, an airstrike from carrier HMS *Victorious* reached *Bismarck*, after being vectored from HMS *Norfolk*. At

LOADING A GERMAN 20.3CM SHELL

Here, the crew of an Admiral Hipper-class cruiser are shown loading a 20.3cm shell inside one of the ship's turrets. Two sailors (**1** and **2**) are manoeuvring an armour-piercing round into the right-side SK C/34 naval gun from the ready-use rack; a third (**3**) disposes of a spent powder cartridge down the cartridge disposal chute. A petty officer (**4**) is supervising them. The crewmen are wearing white utility uniforms, except for the petty officer who wears a blue uniform.

The 8in. main guns of Admiral Hipper-class and British heavy cruisers and the 280mm and 150mm guns on the Deutschland class used separate projectiles and propellant. This required the shell to be inserted first followed by propellant charges. For British cruisers this meant inserting two silk bags each filled with 33lb of cordite. The Germans used two cartridges instead: a cased 71.5kg (157.6lb) main charge and a 36kg (79lb) bagged fore charge for the Deutschlands' 280mm guns, and a 48kg main (105.8lb) charge and a 20kg (44.1lb) fore charge, both cased, for the 203mm guns of the Admiral Hipper-class cruisers.

Separating the projectile and charge slowed loading of the gun. The gun being loaded was lowered to a 3-degree elevation to permit loading. The shell to be loaded, which weighed 122kg (269lb) and came from the shell room (below the turret) or ready-use rack in the turret, was manhandled to the swinging tray, which guided it into the gun's muzzle. The two half charges were then sent up from the magazine and placed in the tray.

A hydraulic rammer moved shell and charges home, and the breech block was sealed. The guns were then elevated to the appropriate angle and fired. After the guns fired, the expended cartridges were removed from the gun barrel, and placed in a disposal chute to remove them from the gun turret.

0130hrs on 25 May, *Prinz Eugen* fired at HMS *Prince of Wales*, preparatory to breaking off from *Bismarck*. HMS *Suffolk* continued tracking *Bismarck*, but lost it two hours later, when *Bismarck* changed course abruptly. Free of British observation, cruiser and battleship separated, *Prinz Eugen* steaming into a North Atlantic cruise, *Bismarck* to France.

En route, *Bismarck* encountered the British Home Fleet, and was sunk in the engagement with battleships HMSs *King George V* and *Rodney*. Heavy cruiser HMS *Dorsetshire* detached itself from a convoy without orders to join the fight, on the principle that no captain can do much wrong if he places his ship alongside that of the enemy. It delivered the final blow, firing three torpedoes at the immobile and disabled *Bismarck*, which sank soon after the torpedoes hit. *Prinz Eugen* made it safely back to France on 1 June, after steaming 14 days without finding any Allied ships.

CODA: THE BARENTS SEA

While 25 May 1941 was the last time German and British heavy cruisers would spar, it was not the end of the war for these ships. Both would continue to battle in the years following. There was even one occasion when they could have fought again, in July 1942.

The occasion was Operation *Rösselsprung* (*Knight's Move*), a plan to trap and destroy an Arctic convoy. It involved all three of Germany's remaining heavy cruisers – *Lützow*, *Admiral Scheer* and *Admiral Hipper* – and the battleship *Tirpitz*. The convoy, PQ 17, had a distant escort including a US and British battleship, two US heavy cruisers and the British County-class heavy cruisers HMSs *London* and *Norfolk*.

The German warships sortied, but returned to port after *Lützow* and three of four destroyers escorting *Tirpitz* ran aground in separate instances. The clash never happened. The convoy was destroyed by U-boats and aircraft after learning *Tirpitz* was at sea.

The last cruiser battle involving Kriegsmarine heavy cruisers occurred six months later on 31 December 1942. Known as the Battle of the Barents Sea or the New Year's Eve Battle, it occurred through an attempt to destroy another Arctic convoy to the Soviet Union, Operation *Regenbogen* (*Rainbow*). This time the target was convoy JW 51B, which had distant cover from two light cruisers, HMSs *Sheffield* and *Jamaica*. *Lützow* and *Admiral Hipper* were dispatched with escorting destroyers.

The plan was for *Admiral Hipper* to attack the convoy first, with *Lützow* holding off until *Admiral Hipper* drew off the escorts. The cruisers' commanders were under orders not to hazard their ships.

The initial part of the plan worked. *Admiral Hipper* and its destroyers fought a spirited action against the British destroyers escorting the convoy. *Lützow* tentatively went after the unprotected convoy, refusing to enter a snow flurry in which the convoy hid. Just as it was starting to attack, the British light cruisers arrived.

These were large light cruisers, each mounting 12 6in. main guns. They were also equipped with accurate gunnery-control radar. They caught *Admiral Hipper* by surprise, attacking its disengaged side. *Admiral Hipper*'s first warning of danger was

when the first – and accurately fired – 6in. shells began landing around it. Several hit, damaging *Admiral Hipper*. It broke off the action.

Lützow had found the convoy and was moving to attack, when it received word *Admiral Hipper* was under fire, and then that *Admiral Hipper* was breaking off the action. Five minutes later, *Lützow* received orders to break off as well. The German cruisers headed home.

The result was a humiliating Kriegsmarine defeat, even if the butcher's bill was even. The Germans sank one British destroyer, badly damaged another and sank a minesweeper. Against this, they suffered damage to *Admiral Hipper* and lost one destroyer. The latter had steamed up to HMS *Sheffield* thinking it was *Admiral Hipper*. In turn, HMSs *Sheffield* and *Jamaica* were so intent on attacking *Admiral Hipper* they noticed their new destroyer companion only when it formed on them. They promptly sank it.

Kriegsmarine heavy cruisers had run from a seemingly weaker force. They ran because they were ordered by Hitler not to hazard their ships. That did not matter to Hitler, who saw the battle as evidence of Kriegsmarine cowardice and incompetence. He ordered the surface fleet scrapped.

The Battle of the Barents Sea, fought on New Year's Eve during the perpetual night of the Arctic winter, was the last surface action in which Kriegsmarine heavy cruisers participated. Their opponents were Royal Navy destroyers and light cruisers. The Kriegsmarine came off worse in the encounter. (USNHHC)

ANALYSIS

The four battles this book examines should be analyzed in two ways: how they were fought, and why they were fought the way they were. All four exchanges between German heavy cruisers and British cruisers shared similar characteristics. They were fought at relatively long ranges, and four were broken off by German forces.

Long ranges meant relatively few hits by both sides. At the Battle of the River Plate, *Admiral Graf Spee* fired between 360 and 390 280mm rounds during the clash. Of these, seven shells hit HMS *Exeter*, one 280mm hit HMS *Ajax*, and *Ajax* and *Achilles* each experienced one very near miss close enough to create damage. German fire was frequently close. Three 280mm salvos straddled HMS *Ajax* early in the battle without doing damage. *Admiral Graf Spee* also fired two salvos at HMS *Achilles* after breaking off combat to warn the shadowing HMS *Achilles* off. The rounds, fired at 23,000yd, landed sufficiently close to HMS *Achilles* to make *Achilles* turn away under cover of smoke.

Still, only ten rounds caused damage, with only eight striking. This yielded only a 2.5–3.5 per cent hit ratio. *Admiral Graf Spee*'s secondary fire was even worse. While its secondary batteries kept HMSs *Achilles* and *Ajax* under fire most of the battle, their fire inflicted no significant damage on the British light cruisers. This implies none of these shots struck. A 150mm shell hitting lightly protected cruisers would have disabled something.

The 300kg 280mm rounds did terrible damage when they struck. Direct hits knocked out two of HMS *Exeter*'s three turrets. Another resulted in severe flooding forward, causing HMS *Exeter* to take on a 7-degree starboard list. The sixth hit, amidships, knocked out internal communications, forcing HMS *Exeter*'s last working turret, its aft one, to go to local control. The sole hit on HMS *Ajax* destroyed its third turret, and knocked the fourth turret out of action.

The incomplete KMS *Seydlitz* (indicated by the arrow) photographed in the Westhaven basin of the Dechimag shipyard in Bremen in May 1942. While largely complete at this time, it was never finished, even after a half-hearted attempt to convert it to an aircraft carrier. (USNHHC)

British fire was equally poor. HMS *Exeter* fired around 210 8in. rounds, landing two hits on *Admiral Graf Spee*. HMSs *Ajax* and *Achilles* between them fired 2,065 6in. rounds, achieving 18 hits. While they created spectacular superficial damage, only one of the 20 British hits did significant damage: an 8in. shell from HMS *Exeter*, which hit the oil purifier. Additionally, British cruisers fired ten torpedoes at *Admiral Graf Spee*, all of which missed. The low percentage of hits occurred despite optimal visual conditions for a daytime gunnery battle and aerial spotting by the British.

Admiral Graf Spee's armour did good service. The 8in. shell that damaged the oil purifier penetrated *Admiral Graf Spee*'s side armour, but burst on the inner armoured deck without penetrating. Three 6in. shells bounced off turret armour of *Admiral Graf Spee*'s main guns without doing damage. A few 150mm and anti-aircraft guns were knocked out, but that was all.

Marksmanship during the Christmas Day Battle was almost as ineffective. *Admiral Hipper* fired 174 main rounds, and an unknown, but probably comparable, number of secondary 105mm rounds. The fire was radar-guided. Despite that, *Admiral Hipper* landed only four hits on HMS *Berwick* and three (probably 105mm rounds) on SSs *Empire Trooper* and *Arabistan*. This was a hit rate of between 2.5 and 3.5 per cent, the same as achieved by *Admiral Graf Spee*. *Admiral Hipper* fired six torpedoes, all at long range. All of them missed, even though they were not evaded, because the British were unaware they had been fired.

British gunnery was even worse, but more understandable given the miserable visibility during the battle. HMS *Berwick* fired 44 salvos, between 184 and 350 rounds, without hitting *Admiral Hipper* once. HMS *Dunedin* did not fire (one reason

Admiral Hipper might have thought it a destroyer), while HMS *Bonaventure* fired 438 rounds without hitting (and apparently without drawing *Admiral Hipper*'s notice). The poor performance was due to the inability of the British to obtain accurate ranges, given the distance and rain.

Neither side landed hits in the cruiser exchanges during the action in the Denmark Strait. This was understandable given the extreme ranges and short durations of the individual gunnery exchanges during the battle. HMSs *Suffolk* and *Norfolk* had no business mixing it up with *Bismarck*, and *Prinz Eugen* had no intention of closing in to fight them without *Bismarck*.

British cruiser gunnery during the Battle of the Barents Sea was highly effective. This time the cruisers engaged were using radar-directed gunnery, and using it to good effect. *Admiral Hipper* received damage before it could respond, including a

Despite relatively minor damage received during the Battle of the River Plate, *Admiral Graf Spee*'s captain chose to scuttle the warship rather than risk the return voyage to Germany. This shows *Admiral Graf Spee*'s magazines exploding after the scuttling charges were detonated and the ship set on fire. (AC)

penetrating hit below the waterline (and below its armour belt). As it finally began to respond to British fire, it received two more hits. These convinced it to break off the action.

This was the other common thread in all four encounters: German cruisers breaking off the action. With HMS *Exeter* crippled and HMS *Ajax* damaged, *Admiral Graf Spee* fled to Montevideo. *Admiral Hipper*, with a troop convoy under its guns, disengaged soon after becoming aware the convoy was protected by a County-class heavy cruiser. *Prinz Eugen* sparred with HMSs *Norfolk* and *Suffolk* at long distance, and eventually broke off. *Admiral Hipper* and *Admiral Scheer* fled after being surprised by two light cruisers.

By contrast, the British attacked or maintained contact in all four battles, despite poor odds in every case. At River Plate, the British disengaged only after two of the three cruisers were damaged and only after being certain *Admiral Graf Spee* was heading to a port where it could be trapped. HMSs *Berwick*, *Sheffield* and *Jamaica* ended the pursuit of their foes due to other responsibilities: to protect convoy WS 5A for HMS *Berwick*, and convoy JW 51B for the other two. Finally, HMSs *Norfolk* and *Suffolk* were charged with shadowing *Bismarck*, not fighting *Prinz Eugen*.

This had less to do with the courage of the respective commanders than the culture of each navy and the training received by both.

While Kriegsmarine heavy cruisers saw significant action during World War II, they rarely fought other heavy cruisers. This shows the *Admiral Hipper* in combat during the 1940 Norway campaign. (USNHHC)

On paper, the quality of individual Kriegsmarine ships and personnel exceeded their Royal Navy counterparts. The Royal Navy had to be less discriminating in choosing personnel than the Kriegsmarine due to its larger size. The Royal Navy needed multiple smaller cruisers to meet its many responsibilities, while the Kriegsmarine, limited in size by treaty, could build the biggest and best in their class.

Yet the Kriegsmarine's weakness lay in its select nature. Its primary purpose was to serve as a fleet in being. It tied down a disproportionate share of Royal Navy resources by existing. The Kriegsmarine had very few ships. The loss of any large ship cost it a disproportionate fraction of its power. When the war started, the Kriegsmarine had two fast battleships, one heavy cruiser and six light cruisers in commission. Only two more battleships and two of the four heavy cruisers under construction joined the fleet during the war, all before 1941 ended. Growth was concentrated in light units, especially U-boats.

After the loss of *Admiral Graf Spee*, Kriegsmarine captains and officers put to sea knowing they were responsible for half of the Kriegsmarine's remaining battleships, battlecruisers and *Panzerschiffe* or heavy cruisers. A captain's primary responsibility was the preservation of his command. Royal Navy captains and officers put to sea expecting to fight, even when the odds were against them.

Under great stress, especially combat, people revert to training. The body shuts down functions unessential to survival while sharpening those most necessary. Among those shut down are memory and higher-level thinking. Action becomes instinctive and not deliberated. Men behave as they have been trained to behave. Once in combat, the British and German officers commanding the ships in these battles reverted to training. German captains instinctively sought to preserve their ships, to keep them

Surviving County-class cruisers were modified and updated during World War II to reflect the changing mission of heavy cruisers between the 1920s and the 1940s. This shows HMS *London* late in the war. Two funnels have replaced the original three. Radar and additional anti-aircraft have been added, while its aircraft have been removed. (AC)

THE DANGER OF DAMAGE

Few heavy cruisers were sunk by gunfire during surface actions in World War II. An 8in. round hitting a 7,000–12,000-ton warship created major damage, yet unless a lucky hit penetrated a magazine, gunnery was unlikely to destroy a large warship. It could demolish gun turrets, cripple steam turbines and diesel engines and knock out boilers. Hits could devastate command and control on the bridge, and eliminate central range-finding and gunnery control, making it impossible to fight effectively.

Yet shells rarely reduced watertight integrity to a point where damage control could not remove water faster than it came in. It was more likely the ship would be immobilized, unable to fight.

Often damaged cruisers, left unmolested, could repair themselves enough to make it to a friendly port safely. Occasionally, they could be towed home. In hostile waters this was impossible. The ships had to be scuttled, with their crews taken aboard other friendly ships.

This fear haunted the Kriegsmarine. Even minor damage while on a raiding cruise incurred hundreds of miles from a friendly port could prove fatal. It was the main reason Kriegsmarine warships avoided combat with even inferior enemy forces unless German superiority was overwhelming.

Damage to HMS *Exeter* as a result of its encounter with *Admiral Graf Spee*. (AC)

available for the next battle. British captains instinctively placed their ships alongside that of the enemy.

The Royal Navy's pugnacious willingness to fight sometimes cost it dearly. In May 1941, trying to evacuate British troops from Crete, the Royal Navy suffered heavy losses to Nazi aircraft. Admiral Andrew Cunningham was urged by subordinates to end the effort. Cunningham replied: 'It takes the Navy three years to build a new ship … it will take 300 years to build a new tradition,' and continued the evacuation. It led to the loss of HMSs *Prince of Wales* and *Repulse* in December 1941. Instead of preserving them as a fleet in being against the superior Imperial Japanese Navy, the commander of that force pushed them into combat, where they were lost.

Yet more often than not, fighting an enemy who placed its priority on the preservation of its fleet, it led to improbable victories, such as at River Plate and the Barents Sea. Even when the Royal Navy came up on the short end of the damage tally, as they did in the battle between *Admiral Hipper* and HMS *Berwick*, it yielded strategic success. Ultimately, the Kriegsmarine's instinctive shielding of its ships from loss cost it the ships it sought to protect – lost not in surface combat, but through Germany's commander discarding them.

AFTERMATH

By the time the war in Europe ended, only *Prinz Eugen* remained of the German heavy cruisers. The rest were sunk or wrecked. *Admiral Graf Spee* lay off Montevideo. *Blücher* was at the bottom of Oslofjord, the world's only major warship sunk by shore-based torpedoes. *Admiral Scheer* and *Admiral Hipper* were bombed and sunk in Kiel near the end of the war. *Lützow*, née *Deutschland*, was scuttled at Altafjord. The incomplete *Seydlitz* was eventually scuttled at Königsberg. Sister ship *Lützow*, sold to the Soviets unfinished, eventually fought for the Soviet Navy as *Petropavlovsk*. It was scrapped in the 1950s.

None were sunk by another heavy cruiser, not even *Admiral Graf Spee*. That ship was scuttled because its captain was unwilling to hazard another battle with imagined battlecruisers lying in wait for it outside Montevideo. In reality nothing awaited except the lone County-class heavy cruiser HMS *Cumberland* and two damaged light cruisers – the same odds it faced a week earlier.

Prinz Eugen suffered the grimmest fate. Given to the US Navy as a war prize, the US kept it to deny it to the Soviets. The US neither wanted nor needed the *Prinz Eugen*. In 1946, it was towed to Bikini Atoll in the Pacific, where it was exposed to two atomic bomb tests, air-burst Test Able and underwater Test Baker. Remarkably, it survived both with little structural damage. Towed to Kwajalein, the wreck sank on 22 December 1946.

Britain's heavy cruisers fared little better than their German counterparts. Five were accorded the dignity of death in combat. HMS *York* was disabled and wrecked by Italian explosive boats, then damaged beyond repair by dive-bombers in May 1941. HMS *Exeter* was sunk by Japanese gunfire in the Java Sea on 1 March 1942. The County-class HMAS *Canberra* was damaged by Japanese cruisers at the Battle of Savo Island, and sank the morning after, 9 August 1942. HMSs *Cornwall* and *Dorsetshire*

were both sunk on 5 April 1942 by Japanese carrier aircraft when Japan's Kido Butai raided Ceylon.

Survivors were scrapped after World War II ended. They were the oldest of Britain's treaty cruisers, with primitive air defence capability and retrofitted electronics. They had seen hard use during the war years. It made more sense for Britain to retain its newer big Town- and Colony-class light cruisers instead of its ancient heavy cruisers. HMSs *Berwick*, *Suffolk*, *Kent*, *London*, *Sussex* and *Norfolk* were retired almost immediately after World War II ended, and scrapped between 1948 and 1950.

HMS *Devonshire* was converted to a cadet training ship in 1947. It was retired in 1954 and sold for scrap. Australia kept HMASs *Australia* and *Shropshire* (the latter given to Australia in 1943 to replace HMAS *Canberra*) until 1954. *Australia* was the flagship of the Royal Australian Navy from 1947 until 1954, with HMAS *Shropshire* kept in reserve. Both were then scrapped, with artefacts retained from them. HMS *Cumberland*, *Admiral Graf Spee*'s would-be opponent, survived the longest. In 1949, it was converted to a gunnery test ship, with its main armament removed and replaced by prototype turrets. Afterwards, it was used to test atomic bomb defences. Finally paid off in 1958, it was scrapped the following year.

A bombed-out *Admiral Hipper* photographed in its dry dock in Kiel by Allied occupiers after the end of the war in Europe in May 1945. Bombed while under repair and further damaged, *Admiral Hipper* is unseaworthy, with structural damage aft. (USNHHC)

BIBLIOGRAPHY

The most useful source in researching this book was Alan Raven's *British Cruiser Warfare: The Lessons of the Early War, 1939–1941* (Seaforth Publishing, Barnsley, 2019), followed closely by M. J. Whitley's *German Cruisers of World War II* (Naval Institute Press, Annapolis, MD, 1985), *German Capital Ships of World War II* (Arms and Armour Press, London, 1989) and Norman Friedman's *British Cruisers: Two World Wars and After* (Seaforth Publishing, Barnsley, 2011). The first three gave highly detailed accounts of the battles in which Kriegsmarine and Royal Navy heavy cruisers clashed. Whitley's and Friedman's books provided excellent technical details of the ships that fought them.

There was no single go-to source for information about German and British heavy cruiser battles. Instead information had to be pieced together from a multitude of different sources, some as unusual as a postcard seller with information about the SS *Empire Trooper*. I cannot list all of them in the available space, but I have listed the most important ones. Books marked with an asterisk are available online.

Brown, David K., *Nelson to Vanguard: Warship Design and Development 1923–1945*, Seaforth Publishing, Barnsley, 2012

Campbell, John, *Naval Weapons of World War Two*, Conway Maritime Press Ltd, London, 1985

Konstam, Angus, *The British Sailor of the Second World War*, Shire Publications, Oxford, 2013

Koop, Gerhard and Schmolke, Klaus-Peter, *German Heavy Cruisers of the Admiral Hipper Class: Warships of the Kriegsmarine*, Seaforth Publishing, Barnsley, 2014

——, *Pocket Battleships of the Deutschland Class: Warships of the Kriegsmarine*, Seaforth Publishing, Barnsley, 2014

A Supermarine Walrus is launched from the catapult of a British cruiser. The biplane Walrus was the main seaplane used by Royal Navy cruisers during World War II. While ungainly, the Walrus could handle rougher seas than the Fairey Firefox it replaced. [AC]

Lavery, Brian, *In Which They Served: The Royal Navy Officer Experience in the Second World War*, Naval Institute Press, Annapolis, MD, 2008

Meier, Friedrich, *Kriegsmarine am Feind*, Verlag Erich Klingmammer, Berlin, 1940*

Roskill, S.W., *History of the Second World War, War at Sea, 1939–45*, Vol. I: *The Defensive*, Her Majesty's Stationery Office, London, 1954

Sieche, Erwin F., 'German Naval Radar to 1945, Part I', *Warship*, Vol. VI, pp. 2–10, Conway Maritime Press, London, 1983

——, 'German Naval Radar Detectors', *Warship*, Vol. VII, pp. 195–97, Conway Maritime Press, London, 1983

Skwiot, Miroslaw, *German Naval Guns: 1939–1945*, Naval Institute Press, Annapolis, MD, 2011

Slader, John, *The Fourth Service: Merchantmen at War 1939–45*, New Era Writer's Guild, Dorset, 1995

Williamson, Gordon, *German Seaman 1939–45*, Osprey Publishing, Oxford, 2009

Websites:

http://www.navweaps.com/

http://www.convoyweb.org.uk/

INDEX